MW00675414

Strategic Business Planning: Securing a Future for the Nonprofit Organization

Miriam P. Kluger
William A. Baker
Howard S. Garval

CWLA Press • Washington, DC

CWLA Press is an imprint of the Child Welfare League of America. The Child Welfare League of America (CWLA) is a privately supported, non-profit, membership-based organization committed to preserving, protecting, and promoting the well-being of all children and their families. Believing that children are our most valuable resource, CWLA, through its membership, advocates for high standards, sound public policies, and quality services for children in need and their families.

CHILD WELFARE LEAGUE OF AMERICA, INC.
440 First Street, NW, Third Floor, Washington, DC 20001-2085
E-mail: books@cwla.org

CURRENT PRINTING (last digit)
10 9 8 7 6 5 4 3 2 1

Cover design by Jenny Geanakos

Printed in the United States of America

ISBN # 0–87868-730-0

Library of Congress Cataloging-in-Publication Data

Kluger, Miriam P.
    Strategic business planning : securing a future for the nonprofit
organization / Miriam P. Kluger, William A. Baker, Howard S. Garval.
        p.   cm.
    Includes bibliographical references (p.   ).
    ISBN 0-87868-730-0
    1. Nonprofit organizations--Management.   2. Strategic planning.
  I. Baker, William A. (Albert), 1939-   . II. Garval, Howard
  S.   III. Title.
HD62.6.K553   1998   98-23709
  658.4'012--dc21

Contents

LIST OF FIGURES

LIST OF TABLES

Acknowledgments

As with our earlier book, *Innovative Leadership in the Nonprofit Organization: Strategies for Change*, this book is drawn from our experiences at the Village for Families and Children. We are especially appreciative of the time and energy the agency's leadership team gave to develop our strategic business plan: Brian Charbonneau, Thomas Hebert, Thomas Lipscomb, Jean Long, Abdul-Rahmaan Muhammad, Nelson Rivera, Nelly Rojas Schwan, Betty Thornton, and Sue Wert. Staff member Melissa Cadwallader competently served as the team's total quality facilitator. We are also grateful for the creativity and talents offered by the many Village staff who participated in work teams and reviewed material as the plan was developed.

We would also like to thank the agency's Board of Directors for their encouragement of this undertaking. Board Strategic Planning and Evaluation Committee Chairperson Hyacinth Douglas Bailey and Committee members Bruce Albro and Ronald Norsworthy provided the impetus for the development of our plan. Chairperson of the Board Sally King provided leadership during implementation of the strategic business plan.

Consultant Jeffrey Hughes of the accounting firm of Coopers & Lybrand L.L.P. provided the expertise and experience needed to facilitate this process. Mary Ann O'Neil of the O'Neil Group trained the Village management and staff in total quality management principles that were integrated throughout the development of the strategic business plan.

We are also appreciative of the talents of our editor, Cathy Corder, who thoughtfully reviewed this manuscript and suggested changes to make this book as clear as possible.

And finally, we would like to thank the very special people in our lives, our families: Martin, Daniel, Hannah, and Jocelyn Kluger; Linda, Barbara, Lisa, and Amy Baker; and MaryEllen, Maren, and Lyndsay Garval.

Preface

The book you are about to read chronicles the implementation of strategic business planning in a nonprofit organization—the Village for Families & Children.

Some of the terminology and activities may seem foreign to you. In the past, nonprofit organizations focused on serving their clients and valued cooperation across agencies. They are now challenged to be both cooperative and competitive, as resources shrink and for-profits enter arenas traditionally served by nonprofit agencies. It is a confusing world when organizations are partners and collaborators one day, and competitors the next day.

The impetus for this journey began when Village leaders became increasingly concerned that the agency was not well-positioned for the future. Similar to the situation of other nonprofits, funding from traditional sources was shrinking. There was also a growing challenge to remain financially sound as managed care began placing limits on the type and length of services covered. At the same time, smaller, more nimble organizations were securing grants that the Village had also applied for.

After careful consideration, the authors became convinced that a strategic business plan was needed to assure a future for the agency. (Long used in the corporate arena, the techniques of strategic business planning are now being adapted and implemented in the world of services for children and families.) This book details the various components of a strategic business plan, from mission and vision to strategy development and implementation. The experience of the authors' agency is used to illustrate the application of each component in a nonprofit organization.

As the process is laid out in the following pages, it may seem that too much time is required for careful strategic business planning. This investment, however, will provide a return to the organization that is well worth the time. Healthy human service organizations exist in a continuous state of change. As Boulding* notes, organizations will regularly experience surprise. Strategies will help the organization deal with change and an uncertain future, so that it does not have to be completely dumbfounded. There is no better time than now to begin this important endeavor.

---

* Boulding, K. E. (1990). The meaning of the 21st century. In B.V. Dean & J.C. Cassidy (Eds.), *Strategic management: Methods and studies* (pp. 349-361). New York: Elsevier Science Publishing Company, Inc.

1 Setting the Stage

In order to understand the context in which the strategic business planning described in this book took place, it is important to have some background information about the Village for Families & Children. The Village for Families & Children, or "the Village," is one of the oldest social service, mental health, and child welfare agencies in the country. Located in Connecticut, it traces its roots back to a group of volunteers called the Hartford Female Beneficent Society. These volunteers first gathered in 1809 out of concern for the well-being of young women wandering the streets of Hartford. It was the volunteers' belief that these young women and their children belonged in safe, caring, and nurturing homes, and they set out to find such caregiving families. Thus began the Village's nearly 200 years of service.

In the early years, the agency was an orphanage. Funds were raised in the mid-1920s to build what was called a "cottage plan." The agency's eight new red-brick Tudor buildings offered a more home-like atmosphere and were considered a service advancement in the care of children living outside their homes.

In 1959, the agency's mission changed to one of protecting children from abusive and neglectful care. In subsequent years, other agencies and services were merged or added. These included one of the country's earliest child guidance clinics, family counseling, home matching for the elderly, and family life education programs. In its

1

evolution, the Village also assumed responsibility for child welfare, legal protection, rehabilitation, and child placement services, including legal protection of children, adoption into permanent homes, provision of foster care, and residential treatment. It also provided basic services to indigent families, outpatient mental health services to children and adults, and a variety of social services intended to support strong family functioning. Further, as a leading agency in the provision of these services, it also assumed responsibility for professional training and applied research.

Each alliance or merger broadened the role and responsibility of the agency and created diverse programming that spanned from cradle to grave. All of these services represented a joining of similar but different missions, service models, and organizational cultures. Each alliance also created a diverse set of cultures within the agency. The cultures within the child welfare, child guidance, and family services areas, for example, were distinctly different.

In many ways, the Village is a leader in its community. It is an agency that is innovative in developing new approaches and takes great pride in the quality of its professional services. Connecticut leaders in child psychiatry, psychology, and social work credit the agency for the success of their careers. In addition, the research and planning department, which is staffed with Ph.D.-level researchers, provides an avenue for research and dissemination that enhances the agency's national reputation.

Generous private giving and a handsome endowment have enhanced the ability of the Village to develop this kind of organization over the years. Discretionary resources, for example, have enabled the agency to make professional investments not financially possible at most private community agencies.

These aspects of the agency's history influenced the "culture" of the organization and shaped the fabric and paradigms for agency operation and planning as the 1980s ended and the 1990s began. This then, was the culture that would need to adapt to rapidly changing human service and health care priorities and strained funding systems.

It has been documented that organizations throughout the world are undergoing major changes [Kilbourne et al. 1996; Kanter 1991; Offerman & Gowing 1990]. Organizational structures have been reinvented, customer and employment relationships have changed, and Total Quality Management (TQM) efforts have been implemented. In an earlier book [Kluger & Baker 1994], the authors described some of the strategies used to navigate this period of change. This book continues where the earlier book left off, describing the development and implementation of an all-encompassing strategic business plan. This kind of planning was and is considered crucial to the survival and growth of the Village and other nonprofit organizations.

Prior to embarking on the strategic business planning process, the Village underwent a major reorganization; that process is described in the following sections.

AGENCY REORGANIZATION

Healthy human service organizations exist in a continuous state of change, which may be expressed in the periodic development of new products, introduction of a new treatment modality, or strengthening of an administrative function. In reality, few organizations challenge their fundamental existence. While the for-profit community favors such terms as "re-invention" or "re-engineering" [Morris & Brandon 1993], nonprofit organizations quickly interpret these words to mean a reaction to economic pressures and business uncertainties. For some, strong negative emotion is quickly attached to the terms. So, rather than use these words, the Village sought to create a fundamentally different organization. This organization would be grounded on a clearer understanding of what the agency existed to achieve and would focus on the ends, rather than the means.

Change or evolution is not new to an organization that traces its roots back to 1809. As was the case with the Village, most established organizations can most assuredly point to "defining moments" in their history. Redefining change, however, consists of episodic events that span periods of years, not months. In the case of the Village, the most recent period of redefining organizational change spanned a period of at least six years. At that, it was still a concentrated period of "defining moments."

One defining moment occurred during a meeting with all agency supervisors and management. The purpose of the meeting was to develop a list of operational barriers that were later to be identified as primary environmental "change drivers." Here, then, are the emerging issues or key reasons why the Village underwent a reorganization:

- ✔ Grant awards were being made to other, often smaller, agencies;

- ✔ The Village held census-based per diem contracts and was not receiving referrals necessary to make the numbers work;

- ✔ The leadership believed that the agency was not able to adequately leverage the Village's strengths;

- ✔ Traditional funding sources were in decline;

- ✔ Mental health priorities were weakening; and

- ✔ There was major customer malaise.

As management reviewed information about the Village position in a changing environment, it became increasingly committed to the importance of leading the agency through a period of fundamental change.

The process began in earnest with a two-day retreat, during which leadership mapped out what was meant by change. Each participant came prepared with written ideas and structures they thought would better organize the agency to deal with the emerging issues. Leadership shared several reorganization goals, discussed below.

Goal #1: Customer Responsiveness

All leadership at the retreat felt that the new organization should be more responsive to its customers. Leadership drew a distinction between customers and clients. Customers was considered the broader term, encompassing both clients and external customers, the former being the direct recipients of services, and the latter representing the external customer, such as a funder, organization, or individual who referred to the agency. Customers also included the internal customers, or staff within the organization. Participants emphasized the importance of treating one another with respect, as would be the practice with a paying customer.

The Village's increased involvement in providing community- or neighborhood-based services also made the term "client" inappropriate in many instances. Unlike a traditional mental health program, individuals served by prevention and family support programs don't have to have a problem in order to receive services. A participant at a school-based family resource center, for example, would not aptly be referred to as a client.

It was further agreed that there would be zero tolerance for customer and consumer disdain. Customers were viewed as at the top of the organizational hierarchy. This viewpoint is often referred to as an inverted or upside-down pyramid [Albrecht 1992]. From this perspective, everything is seen as existing in order to support the client. In addition, a further commitment was also made to serve the external customer, which meant being more responsive to referring organizations, such as installing a direct telephone line to the agency for a key external customer/referral source.

Goal #2: Community-Based Service Development

The agency traditionally provided office-based services at its main campus and conducted outreach into schools and other community organizations. It was determined that service programs had to become more a part of the neighborhood. The services needed to go to where the families lived and went to school, rather than have the families come to the agency campus. Community-based also meant taking more of the lead from the community and not just being physically in the neighborhood.

Goal #3: Client and Staff Empowerment

Because many of the individuals served by the agency came involuntarily, it was all too easy to define for them what they needed. It was considered critical that staff more systematically engage even involuntary clients in the determination of what services were needed. The agency could also develop performance measures that focused on building family capacity and articulating expected outcomes.

Goal #4: Providing Holistic Family Services

Leadership believed that the Village needed to make its system of services more responsive to the multiple needs of its consumers. New structures would have to provide multidisciplinary assessment, planning, case management, and delivery of customized, comprehensive services that focused on the whole family. To improve a child's life, improvements and changes also had to be made in the caregiver's life.

Goal #5: Expanded Collaboration

Leadership believed that systems of care would be increasingly important to such customers as managed care organizations. This would require greater collaboration across agency services, as well as with other organizations. While collaborations generally require more time, they are necessary to successfully serve the family with multiple needs.

In addition to these five goals, the leadership team became increasingly convinced that the agency needed a culture that embraced and, in fact, thrived on change. This did not refer to innovation, which some had previously thought of as change. Most certainly, it required that the leadership of the agency actively lead change and continuously reiterate goals and agency direction. The team also concluded that staff should be provided with an opportunity to participate and manage change, thereby making the process and outcome less threatening. In order to secure the future, the leadership team expressed unanimous support to organizationally restructure the agency consistent with these goals.

The retreat concluded with the establishment of a common vision that "all families served by the agency would achieve a level of self-sufficiency that would enable them to independently provide for the emotional and economic, social, and developmental needs of members, and that the agency would provide self-sufficient families for children who would otherwise fall outside of permanent, nurturing families."

Within 60 days, a joint leadership and supervisory staff retreat was held, because obtaining middle managers' buy-in and support and garnering agencywide consensus were necessary for success in such major change. Attendees came up with the same results in establishing goals and also concluded that change and upheaval were undoubtedly operational realities for the near future.

Participants in the second retreat also concluded that all staff should have an opportunity to give input on goals for the future. Using an abbreviated retreat format, they identified similar goals at this retreat. Supervisors planned and carried out the half-day meetings that included all the agency staff.

The outcome of similar conclusions from three different levels of staff (leadership, supervisors, line staff), leant further credence that the goals selected were the right goals. Thus, at the conclusion of these retreats the agency had developed a common set of goals for change and consensus about the need to materially change the way the agency structured its management and carried out its business:

✔ Improve customer response,

✔ Emphasize community-based service development,

✔ Empower clients and staff,

✔ Respond to the holistic needs of client families, and

✔ Expand internal and external collaboration.

These common goals came to be referred to as the agency's five operational strategies, and they became the groundwork for the changes ahead. Consensus among the planning participants about what the organization's operational strategies should be was critical, because these beliefs or values would underlie decisions made throughout the strategic business planning process [Kaufman 1992].

Follow-up leadership meetings focused on considering a mission change for the agency. These meetings also considered a new model for an operational structure that would address the barriers to change identified earlier and that would support the achievement of the five operational strategies which had been set for the agency. In addition, principles of Total Quality Management [Deming 1986], which will be discussed in the next chapter, significantly influenced the processes within the organization. For example, there was a belief that broad, full staff participation in the change process was necessary, as was use of stronger problem-solving skills and fostering of internal collaboration.

NEW MODEL FOR OPERATIONAL STRUCTURE

Reorganizing the operational structure and management of the agency became the next priority. The members of the current leadership gave some thought as to how the management of the organization might be changed. Now it was time to sift through individual ideas and develop specific strategies.

The leadership team shared the goal that this planning would yield a structure which would support the five operational strategies. That is, the structure would need to meet the criteria of improving customer response, emphasizing community-based service development, empowering clients and staff, internal and external collaboration, and responding to the holistic needs of the children and families the agency served. As was the case for the Village, changes in strategies frequently require changes in the organizational structure [David 1993].

The leadership team recognized that the planning could mean a change in job assignments and that these changes might not be viewed as ideal by the leader affected. To encourage full participation in the planning process, it was essential that team members at least be given assurances of a future job without a salary reduction.

The organizational charts in Figure 1 show the former and new structure. Note that in the former structure, leaders responsible for both line and staff functions reported directly to the President. In the new structure, an Administrative Leadership Team was established to oversee all of the key staff functions of the organization. This new structure also streamlined leadership reporting directly to the President, enabling the President to devote more time to fundraising and networking on behalf of the Village.

The new structure also indicates a new Program Leadership Team, led by the Executive Vice President and Chief Operating Officer. The team consists of leaders with program responsibilities and the Senior Vice President for Research and Planning. This latter function was included in the Program Leadership Team, rather than the administrative team, in recognition of the importance of associating outcome measures directly with agency services. It was recognized that the Senior Vice President for Research and Planning would also lead agencywide planning efforts that included the Administrative Leadership Team—including strategic business planning.

One drawback to the earlier structure was that the divisions pigeonholed leaders and leadership perspective, resulting in a rigid hierarchy. A goal of the reorganization was to establish a more fluid structure, with leadership responsible for both clinical and preventive community programs. The new structure was an effort to show appreciation for a holistic continuum of care, despite the discouragement of such by rigid, categorical funding. The staff viewpoint—that the program entered was the only service a family needed—had to be broadened.

The new structure also attempted to ameliorate any gulf that traditionally exists between staff and line functions. The new position

Figure 1. Organizational Charts Reflecting Former and New Structure

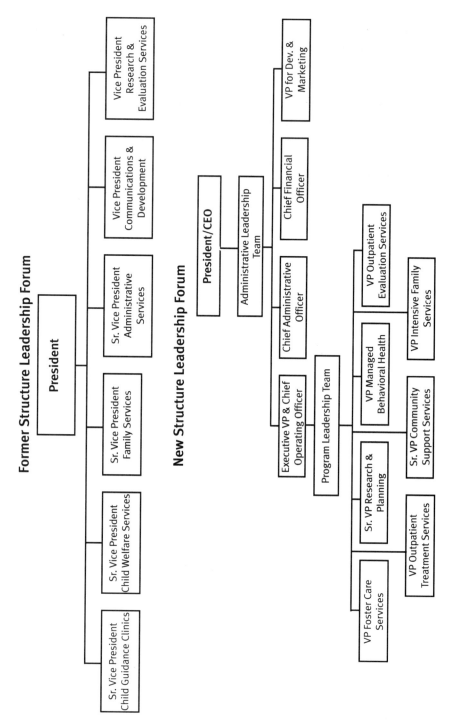

Former Structure Leadership Forum

New Structure Leadership Forum

of Executive Vice President was developed, with the responsibility and authority to coordinate planning and problem solving between line leaders and staff leaders. It was anticipated that this would materially help to lower a perception that the balance of power favored staff functions. It also simultaneously enhanced expectations that line and staff leadership had to effectively negotiate with one another in order to be successful. It quickly became apparent that neither could plan in isolation of the other.

The Combined Leadership Team (CLT) was formed to jointly guide the agency through the change process. The CLT consisted of both the Administrative and Program Leadership Teams. The term "team" was initially a misnomer—it took nearly a year for the group to gel into a working unit after a teambuilding effort and shared participation in planning. In addition, managed care readiness required that the two areas work together to successfully participate in Medicaid Managed Care. Over time, however, the CLT became the preferred group for agencywide budgeting, program planning, and problem solving. It now meets more frequently than the individual Program and Administrative Leadership Teams.

Table 1 on the next page summarizes the former organization and the attributes desired after the reorganization. Note that, while these qualities were identified particularly for the authors' organization, many of them have application to other large, multiservice organizations.

The Role of the Board of Directors in the Reorganization

Discussion of a reorganization is not complete without a review of the role of the Board of Directors in such a process. For any fundamental change to occur, the Board of Directors must be equally passionate about the need for change. Just prior to the effort to ready management and staff for material organizational change, the Board of Directors had been engaged in an examination of organizational needs and barriers to change. An organizational mandate that emphasized adherence of the agency to the work with which it had the

Table 1. Comparison of Attributes of Former and New Organizational Structure

FORMER STRUCTURE	NEW STRUCTURE
Services drive mission	Mission drives services
Structure not relevant to evolving service delivery needs	Structure is dictated by service delivery needs
Squeeze clients into categorical services	Services meet client/customer needs
Discrete services	More holistic services
Barriers to being community-based	Community-based
Not optimally proactive with funders	Proactive with funders, clients
Difficult to explain to potential donors what agency does	Easier to explain to potential donors what agency does
Competition between divisions	No competition
Turf protection, identify with own program	Greater sense of ownership, identify with agency
"(service) clients"	"agency clients"
Not full appreciation/understanding of how parts fit into whole	Appreciation/understanding of how parts fit into whole
Collaboration more difficult	Collaboration easier
Rigid structure	Fluid, flexible structure
Sustaining, preserving past	Nimble, fast, innovative
Individual talents not optimally used	Readily draw on individual talents
Financial and human resources not optimally used	Effective use of financial and human resources
Duplication, high administrative overhead	Leaner organization

greatest experience and expertise came from work done by the Board of Directors Strategic Planning and Evaluation Committee. In addition, the Board insisted that the organization become less diversified and more focused. It was also leadership's belief that a more focused organization would have a better chance of establishing its value in an increasingly competitive environment. In addition, leadership believed that greater focus would have a positive impact on the agency's key stakeholders and image development. This new focus meant that the Village needed to move away from serving the elderly and single adults and move toward creating a niche in children's services, a niche where the Village would be the dominant player.

A mission statement was adopted that articulated the organization's intended outcome of fewer children abused and a reduction of violence within families. This new mission statement broke from the agency's broad traditional mission that spoke of providing social and mental health services to a more-focused mission statement that emphasized the agency's anticipated outcomes.

REFERENCES

Albrecht, K. (1992). *At America's service: How corporations can revolutionize the way they treat their customers.* New York: Warner Books, Inc.

David, F. R. (1993). *Strategic management* (4th ed.). New York: Macmillan Publishing Company.

Deming, W. E. (1986). *Out of the crisis.* Cambridge, MA: Massachusetts Institute of Technology Center for Advanced Engineering Study.

Kanter, R. M. (1991). Transcending business boundaries: 12,000 world managers view change. *Harvard Business Review, 69* (3), 151-164.

Kaufman, R. (1992). *Strategic planning plus: An organizational guide.* Newbury Park, CA: Sage Publications.

Kilbourne, L. M., O'Leary-Kelly, A. M., & Williams, S. D. (1996). Employee perceptions of fairness when human resource systems change: The case of employee layoffs. In R. W. Woodman & W. A. Pasmore (Eds.), *Research in organizational change and development* (pp. 25-48). Greenwich, CT: Jai Press, Inc.

Kluger, M. P., & Baker, W. A. (1994). *Innovative leadership in the nonprofit organization: Strategies for change.* Washington, DC: Child Welfare League of America.

Morris, D. C., & Brandon, J. (1993). *Re-engineering your business.* New York: McGraw-Hill, Inc.

Offerman, L. R., & Gowing, M. K. (1990). Organizations of the future: Changes and challenges. *American Psychologist, 45,* 95-108.

2 Why a Strategic Business Plan?

Change occurs constantly and given this reality, the formidable task for organizations is to focus on the *content* of change rather than the *degree* of change [Sanno 1992]. At the end of 1992, senior management at the Village were becoming increasingly concerned that the agency was not well-positioned for the future. A number of trends or events contributed to this concern:

- ✔ Funding from traditional sources, such as the United Way, was shrinking. In addition, there was a growing challenge to remain financially sound in the outpatient mental health services area as managed care began placing limits on the type and length of the services it would cover.

- ✔ Smaller, more nimble organizations were securing grants that the Village had also applied for. Several of these successful agencies were more grassroots-oriented and community-based than the Village was at that time.

- ✔ The need to collaborate with others was becoming an increasingly important issue for both funders and the community. The Village's ability to collaborate needed to improve at both the internal and external level.

Another impetus for deciding to develop a strategic business plan came from the Board of Directors. Prior to the development of the strategic business plan, the Board's Strategic Planning and Evaluation Committee, a group made up of business executives, addressed the question: Was something missing in the current strategic plan, or was it complete as is? The Committee concluded that the agency's mission, strategic priorities, and operational strategies were still on target and the right focus for the Village. The Committee also determined, however, that a review of the Village's competition and the position of the agency in the marketplace was missing. The Village also needed financial and competitive information to round out its planning. The Committee encouraged the agency to combine all the independent planning endeavors into one cohesive plan that would clarify whether any other pieces were missing.

While the Village had been involved in strategic planning for nearly a decade, the Combined Leadership Team, or CLT, elected to develop a strategic business plan that would secure the agency's benchmark position in services to children and families. In particular, the Village chose to develop a strategic business plan with the following goals:

- ✔ To assure a future;

- ✔ To determine where to go (visions with values), how to get there (strategies), and to achieve agency visions;

- ✔ To seek a financially sound future at an extremely uncertain time;

- ✔ To leverage the agency endowment;

- ✔ To be successful at what the agency does;

- ✔ To be timely in response to opportunities;

- ✔ To be ahead of the curve, on the cutting edge; and

- ✔ To be proactive, rather than reactive.

The planning process took place during a five-month period. The process differed from previous agency planning in several ways:

- ✔ Borrowing a practice from the business world, the CLT grouped the current and anticipated agency programs and services into four **lines of business:** Intensive Children's Services, Managed Behavioral Health Services, Neighborhood and Family Strengthening Services, and Workplace Services. Lines of business are one way of organizing service products that naturally go together, because they have distinct markets and customers. For example, the service products within the Intensive Children's Services line of business shared several characteristics:

- They are the most intensive level of care at the Village,
- They serve abused children who have been removed from their biological home or who are at risk of removal,
- They are funded by the state department of children and families, and
- They are viewed as hospital/institutional diversion programs.

This approach provided a framework for internal and external constituents (including managed care companies) to understand the agency's many programs. In particular, it was helpful to Board members from the business world, who found thinking in terms of lines of business compatible with their own experiences.

✔ **Use of "visioning" was expanded** to complement the agency's mission, lines of business, and value-added services (e.g., research and training programs). Previous visioning that had occurred at the Village was primarily related to management's vision for excellence. Included in the leadership vision, for example, were such ideas as a commitment to change as a process, rather than as an event; commitment to a culturally diverse workforce as crucial to effective community service; and dedication to timely decision making and risk taking.

✔ Every effort was made to base decisions on **objective data** from several sources:

- Information from competitors and funders;
- Information from clients and staff; and
- Financial data, using a financial pro forma format.

✔ **Line staff were involved early** in the planning process. Line staff were selected to join the work groups that had formed to develop plans for a particular line of business, such as Intensive Children's Services. The work groups also included members of the CLT. Presentations and written communications occurred throughout the process, inviting reactions and suggestions. Line staff also acted as representatives of their coworkers and shared material with colleagues on a regular basis. Any concerns or suggestions were shared with either the line of business work group or full planning group as appropriate. When the full planning group met, there were a total of 18 line staff and 12 CLT members.

✔ **A facilitator trained in Total Quality Management (TQM)** was present at the large group meetings. The criteria for selection of a facilitator will be outlined later in this chapter. The facilitator for the strategic business plan had been trained in TQM facilitation techniques, was a line staff person, and was highly respected by the management team and her coworkers. The facilitator worked closely with the lead planner on preparing meetings and reviewing meeting agendas.

✔ **A consultant** experienced in strategic business planning was hired. The reasons for engaging a consultant will be described in greater detail later in this chapter. Overall, the Village felt it was important to receive guidance from someone who had experience with strategic business planning in areas new to the Village (such as a competitive analysis) and with such for-profit concepts as lines of business. The consultant also had experience with integrating planning and financial information.

TOTAL QUALITY MANAGEMENT

One of the tenets that guided the agency's strategic business planning as well as the agency reorganization was Total Quality Management (TQM). TQM, as outlined by Jablonski [1992], is a cooperative way of doing business that incorporates participative management, continuous improvement, and the use of teams. In his book, Jablonski outlines six principles of TQM:

✔ Having a customer focus,

✔ Attending to process in addition to outcome,

✔ Attending to the prevention of poor quality rather than inspection of errors,

✔ Using the expertise of the workforce,

✔ Making decisions based on facts, and

✔ Giving feedback.

With regard to using the expertise of the workforce, TQM emphasizes empowering employees at the most appropriate levels within the organization to make decisions [George & Weimerskirch 1994]. This makes good sense, because employees who are directly involved in providing the service or product are in the best place to know what can be improved.

When senior management made a decision to receive training in TQM, it was recognized that this would be an ongoing, long-term commitment. Movement to a Total Quality Organization first involved examining existing paradigms and consciously adopting new ones. (Paradigms are conceptual frameworks and commonly accepted ideas of a certain group, in this case, the agency staff [Sanno 1992].)

A volunteer of the agency, who was an expert in the TQM field, offered her services to the Village pro bono. All staff received 21 hours of training on a variety of topics:

✔ What TQM is,

✔ What the barriers to quality at the Village are,

✔ Interactive behavior skills,

✔ Approaches and tools for problem solving,

✔ Quality communication, and

✔ Meeting effectiveness.

More than 30 staff with supervisory responsibilities received additional training in managing as a quality leader and more than one dozen staff received training in how to facilitate meetings and problem-solving teams, one of the tools of TQM. The following concepts—facilitators, meeting effectiveness, and accurate and timely data—played a major role throughout the strategic business planning process.

Facilitators

Facilitators are responsible for assuring that the group uses effective processes to get its work done. A facilitator will comment on process, not content, in order to keep the meeting moving along. For example, a facilitator might point out that a question had been raised about whether there was consensus on a particular issue, but that the group had moved on without checking for consensus or responding to the question. Many times meetings are ineffective because decisions don't get made or participants think there was agreement on something, when in fact this was never confirmed. TQM emphasizes consensus decision making, because, if everyone involved can support a decision, then there is good "buy-in" and implementation will be met with less or no resistance. The following were some of the criteria used in selecting staff members to become trained as facilitators [O'Neil 1992]:

- ✔ Respected by peers,

- ✔ Good energy level,

- ✔ Genuine sense of humor,

- ✔ Excellent interactive behavior skills,

- ✔ Good listening skills, and

- ✔ Good organizational skills.

Meeting Effectiveness

Meeting effectiveness includes assignment of attendees to facilitate, keep time, and take notes during a meeting. Associated with each agenda item at the Village is a timeframe, desired outcome, priority, and whether the agenda item is categorized as information sharing, discussion, and/or decision making.

The training placed significant emphasis on team building, meeting effectiveness, and involving staff at the most appropriate level for decision making. Whenever possible, decision making was by consensus rather than majority rule. (Consensus means that there is agreement by two or more people to support a position.) Everyone must live with and support the group's decision, even if the final decision was not the individual's first preference.

Accurate and Timely Data

TQM also emphasizes that effective problem solving and decision making are based on accurate and timely data, rather than on perception, opinion, or experience [Walton 1986].

TQM AND STRATEGIC BUSINESS PLANNING

Ways in Which TQM Was Integrated into the Strategic Business Planning Process

- ✔ Miriam Kluger, one of the authors of this book, was the Village's lead planner for the strategic business planning

process. While the lead planner was responsible for overall coordination of the effort, a staff member who had been
trained in meeting facilitation assumed the **facilitation** role
during large group meetings. She worked closely with the
lead planner on planning meetings and establishing the
meeting agendas.

✔ The CLT developed the agencywide vision for the Village.
In accordance with **empowering employees at the most
appropriate levels** within the organization to make decisions, visions for each of the lines of business were developed by line staff in collaboration with CLT members
responsible for that area. Visions were only accepted when
full support, or consensus, was reached. Consensus decision making was also used at other times during the strategic planning process, as deemed appropriate.

✔ CLT members identified and invited **line staff** to participate in the work groups that met within each line of business. All of the strategies were developed within these work
groups, functioning in a manner similar to self-directed
work teams. These strategies formed the core of the strategic business plan. Line staff and CLT members all contributed to the generation of ideas for these strategies. CLT
members did not have any more decision-making influence than line staff in strategy selection. This made sense,
since line staff and leadership each bring a valuable perspective to how the agency should position itself for the
future. It was not a case where line staff or leadership would
have been the better decision makers.

✔ The **TQM meeting effectiveness tools**, such as meeting
agendas with defined goals, roles, and processes; time
frames for each agenda item; desired outcome for each item;
preparation needed before the meeting, etc., were all used
regularly as part of this planning process. Effective brain-

storming was also emphasized. All ideas were accepted and no one was allowed to comment on or critique a particular idea during the brainstorming process. Participants could, of course, build on another's idea.

✔ One tenet of TQM is that effective problem solving is based on fact, rather than on perception or opinion. The Village's strategic business planning **emphasized data gathering** as an important element in the planning and decision-making processes. Data, for example, were used to determine target markets and to understand trends in agency services, in the human service marketplace, and among competitors. As will be described later, a consultant gathered data directly from competitors through individual interviews.

✔ Once the plan was developed, it was critical to communicate the outcome to all key stakeholders. Effective or **quality communication** is another tenet of TQM and is one critical way to obtain staff support. Engaging all staff in supporting implementation of the strategic business plan was a critical success factor. Staff as a whole needed to understand the rationale for this planning process, the desired outcomes, financial implications, direct effect on staff, implementation plans, and procedures to monitor implementation and measure success. These areas needed to be conveyed without getting mired in details and, where appropriate, staff participation was invited.

✔ The **Board of Directors** and Board Strategic Planning and Evaluation Committee needed to be kept informed of progress during the development of the plan. Communication was extremely important to this constituency, as the plan needed to comply with the mandate that the organization become less diversified and more focused.

TQM skills served the Village well during a planning process that was time intensive, challenging, and occasionally ambiguous.

Ways in Which TQM Was Integrated into the Reorganization

TQM principles also influenced the reorganization process. Consensus, for example, was required for certain decisions. TQM was an especially important influence in the establishment of self-directed work teams.

Self-Directed Service Teams

A discussion of the new model for operational structure would not be complete without mention of the self-directed service teams and the reason for their development. Unlike the former structure, the new structure eliminated the supervisor's group, the Village's middle management layer. These responsibilities were assumed by the Program Leadership Team, in addition to their other, broader, leadership responsibilities. The new structure also merged the children and adult outpatient service divisions. The two divisions were housed in separate buildings and had separate cultures. In integrating the two divisions into one, leadership thought it critical to break up the physical barrier of separate buildings. This was accomplished through the formation of self-directed service teams, sometimes referred to as self-directed work teams [George & Weimerskirch 1994].

The Executive Vice President and the Program Leaders responsible for outpatient services determined the membership of the self-directed service teams. Influenced by the TQM training that was going on at the same time, these self-directed or self-managed work teams chose an internal, full-time member to be their leader. The team also had responsibility in such areas as training, goal setting, and evaluating the team's performance [Sims & Lorenzi 1992].

With regard to the composition of the self-directed service teams, it was decided that each team should have a mix of staff members from each of the two divisions to help facilitate the merger. Other considerations included diversity of culture, gender, bilingual skills, and special skills in the areas of child sexual abuse, substance abuse, violence, and brief treatment. Part-time staff were also divided among the teams.

The ability of the teams to be self-directive was especially important, given the elimination of the middle management layer. Before team leaders were selected, each team underwent a teambuilding process facilitated by the Village's TQM consultant. These kinds of teams typically select their own leader. Leadership, however, does approximately the same amount of work as the other team members; leaders do not, for example, delegate unpleasant tasks [Katzenbach & Smith 1993]. The criteria for team leader were developed by leadership with input from the outpatient staff and the TQM consultant:

- ✔ Good relationships with teammates and others throughout the agency;

- ✔ Flexibility;

- ✔ Appreciation for the team approach;

- ✔ Strong, effective interactive behavior skills;

- ✔ Ability to perform a number of the jobs performed by other team members;

- ✔ Strong organizational skills; and

- ✔ Full-time employee of the agency.

The teams identified their functions and assigned a member to lead that function. Functions identified by outpatient service teams included liaison with client intake and case assignment. The program leadership for outpatient services periodically met with the team leaders to address issues that emerged during implementation. Because of the elimination of middle management, there was some initial confusion among team leaders that they were supervisors. They were periodically reminded that only the program leaders had supervisory responsibilities. Further, peer supervision triads within the service teams were established to address clinical supervision needs previously addressed by middle managers.

INFLUENCE OF MANAGED CARE

Nonprofit organizations felt the influence of managed care as early as 1990. (Managed care organizations [MCOs] strive to provide the most appropriate services in a cost-effective manner that leads to both optimal outcomes and satisfied service recipients and providers [HCFA 1994].) Nonprofit organizations began entering into contracts with MCOs, particularly in the area of outpatient services. MCOs are also expanding to encompass child welfare services [Seelig & Pecora 1996].

Connecticut's recent move to public sector managed care, in particular Medicaid Managed Care, affected nearly 80% of the Village's outpatient clients. This trend, reviewed in Chapter 6 (see page 68), caused leadership to realize that managed care contracts were becoming the only vehicle through which Village clients could be served.

The explosion of managed care meant that the Village would increasingly be operating in a highly competitive environment and doing more business with for-profit companies, such as health maintenance organizations and MCOs. These companies are oriented to the bottom line, and the cost of services is a dominant factor. The leadership recognized that the agency would need to adapt to this evergrowing market and demonstrate that it was a viable player.

While the effect of managed care on the Managed Behavioral Health Services line of business was clear, the impact on child welfare services became a growing concern. These services do not fit neatly into the medical model. For example, medical necessity is not as clear cut as it is with outpatient mental health and substance abuse services. The verdict is not yet in on what impact managed care will have on child welfare services. As of this writing, there are a few states, such as Kansas and Massachusetts, that have already privatized their child welfare services under a managed care contract.

ADDITIONAL FEATURES OF THE STRATEGIC BUSINESS PLANNING PROCESS

Use of a Consultant

As mentioned earlier, although the Village had done strategic planning since 1988, the new strategic business plan included such new areas as a competitive analysis, borrowing such for-profit concepts as lines of business and integration of financial information. The Village further believed that someone not directly connected with the agency might be able to obtain market analysis information more readily. The consultant selected would also have expertise in managed care and be able to advise the Village in that area as needed. Several other criteria were used in the selection of the consultant:

✔ Health care orientation,

✔ Belief in creating a vision statement as the first step,

✔ Orientation to competitive threats and opportunities,

✔ Ability to meet Village project deadlines, and

✔ Competitiveness of price.

Other reasons consultants are selected, as identified by Morrus [1984] include objectivity, experience in the area, problem-solving skills, an ability to devote concentrated time to the effort, and the ability to make otherwise politically unacceptable statements or conclusions. Further, consultants are important when the organization lacks time, staff, or a desire to do the planning in-house. They may also structure the process and elicit ideas already existing in the organization.

Preparing the Board of Directors

It was important to prepare the Board of Directors for the many changes to occur at the Village. One way this happened was through the President's and Executive Vice President's presentations to the Board Executive Committee and full Board about managed care principles in general and the agency's involvement in Medicaid Managed Care in particular. Since this represented a majority of the business in the Managed Behavioral Health Services line of business, it was critical that Board members have a good general understanding of managed care and where the agency was in providing service in such an environment.

Communications to Staff, Board Members, and Others

Sharing progress and decisions with agency staff and Board members was an important component of the strategic business planning process. Regular communications in the agency newsletter were published during development and at completion of the plan.

The organization of agency services into lines of business was a useful concept in explaining what, at first glance, appeared to be a confusing array of services. This diagram of the lines of business was especially helpful when trying to explain the relationship and organization of services to a variety of groups:

✔ Funders such as the United Way,

✔ New staff,

✔ Potential or new Board members,

✔ Potential or new collaborating partner organizations,

✔ Program or agency site visitors from accrediting and licensing bodies,

✔ Managed care companies, and

✔ The state's department of children and families.

The President and Executive Vice President went to department meetings to discuss the strategic business plan. Although some line staff were directly involved in the planning process, others needed an opportunity to ask questions and offer suggestions directly to the President and Executive Vice President. Line staff who were part of a work group also spoke at the meetings. It was important for Village staff who were not directly involved in the planning to understand what was going on and to be supportive of the plan.

Because line staff were involved early in the planning process, they were exposed to the debating and uncertainty that occurs during the decision-making process. Some line staff had the perception that the leaders should have all the answers and were somewhat unsettled by seeing that this is not necessarily the case. On a positive note, early involvement allowed line staff in the work groups to be equal partners during the decision-making process.

Another important communication to staff and Board members occurred during the sharing of the agency budget. The presentation showed how lines of business were financially supported, directly linking the budget to the strategics.

The strategic business plan represented a great deal of work and detail. The authors gave a presentation to the Board Strategic Planning and Evaluation Committee prior to the full Board presentation. The Committee provided valuable suggestions on how to most clearly and simply present the results of the effort. For example, rather than attempt to discuss each line of business in any detail, they suggested that an overview be given, followed by a more detailed review of just one of the lines.

An all-staff meeting was held on the topic of the strategic business plan. After being given an update on progress and decisions to date, the larger gathering divided into smaller groups. Members from each of the line of business work groups presented the vision, products, and services within the line and associated strategies. Time was reserved for questions and answers during each of the small group presentations.

COMPONENTS OF A STRATEGIC BUSINESS PLAN

The remaining chapters of this book provide discussion of the components of a strategic business plan:

✔ Developing mission and vision statements,

✔ Describing a line of business,

✔ Leading a situational assessment,

✔ Conducting an external assessment,

✔ Commissioning a competitive analysis,

✔ Allocating discretionary dollars,

✔ Developing and implementing strategies,

✔ Monitoring the strategic business plan, and

✔ Refreshing the strategic business plan.

The Village for Families & Children | The authors believe that strategic business planning is necessary to securing a future for nonprofit organizations. The experiences of the Village are offered as an example of how these components may be applied in a nonprofit setting.

REFERENCES

George, S., & Weimerskirch, A. (1994). *Total quality management: Strategies and techniques proven at today's most successful companies.* New York: John Wiley & Sons, Inc.

Health Care Financing Administration Office of Managed Care [HCFA]. (1994). *Best practices of managed care organizations* (HCFA Publication No. 1994-300-926/23458). Washington, DC: U.S. Government Printing Office.

Jablonski, J. R. (1992). *Implementing TQM: Competing in the nineties through total quality management.* San Diego: Pfeiffer & Company.

Katzenbach, J. R., & Smith, D. K. (1993). *The wisdom of teams: Creating the high-performance organization.* Boston: Harvard Business School Press.

Morrus, S. K. (1984). *Building the strategic plan: Find, analyze, and present the right information.* New York: John Wiley & Sons.

O'Neil, M. (August 2, 1992). Personal communication. The O'Neil Group, 20 Lucy Way, Simsbury, Connecticut.

Sanno Management Development Research Center. (1992). *Vision management: Translating strategy into action.* Cambridge, MA: Productivity Press.

Seelig, W. R., & Pecora, P. J. (1996). The changing world of services for children and families: Reinventions for the 21st century. In P. J. Pecora, W. R. Seelig, F. A. Zirps, & S. M. Davis (Eds.), *Quality improvement and evaluation in child and family services: Managing into the next century* (pp. 3-32). Washington, DC: Child Welfare League of America, Inc.

Sims, H. P. Jr., & Lorenzi, P. (1992). *The new leadership paradigm: Social learning and cognition in organizations.* Newbury Park, CA: Sage Publications, Inc.

Walton, M. (1986). *The Deming management method.* New York: Perigee Books.

3 Developing Mission and Vision Statements

WHAT IS A MISSION?

The mission of a nonprofit organization is the driving force behind service provision and program development. It is the business that the organization is in [Oster 1995] and answers the questions, "Why are we here?" and "Where are we going?" Oster further points out that mission statements may serve three purposes:

✔ To provide boundaries or focus for the organization,

✔ To function as a motivator of both staff and donors, and

✔ To provide criteria for evaluating the success of the organization.

Expressed another way, the mission statement explains two essentials about an organization: what it is and what it does [Falsey 1989].

The mission should be framed in measurable terms that will lead to a clear evaluation of whether it was achieved. The statement may be quite brief, although it must arise from thorough discussions among key stakeholders about the identity and purpose of the organization, core values, and ethical standards [Bryson 1995]. An example of a mission for a child welfare agency might be: "To provide a permanent home for all children in the county who are unable to live with their biological parent(s)."

Process for Developing a Mission Statement

Development of, or change in, a nonprofit organization's mission most likely includes formation of a team of management and Board members. Board members are involved because they are charged with setting organizational direction and for defining the boundaries within which managers and service providers operate. The Board may initiate a change in the organization's mission or vote whether or not to accept a revised mission as recommended by management [Kluger & Baker 1994].

Regardless of who initiates such a process, the team charged with developing a new mission should begin with an examination of the deficits of the existing mission and rationale for amending or abandoning it. It is helpful to list these reasons and use them as a checklist against which to test drafts of new mission statements as they are developed.

Once these reasons have been identified, the team may individually write down their answers to such questions as:

✔ "What is the business that this organization is in?"

✔ "Why are we here?"

✔ "Where are we going?"

Participants can then share their responses with the other team members to generate discussion. The goal of such an exercise is to identify the key elements of why the organization exists.

The mission development team may then develop and discuss drafts of mission statements that incorporate aspects from several participant suggestions. The criteria that were previously agreed upon are then used to assess the viability or goodness of fit of the mission statement. Thus, the mission statements should be reviewed to assure that deficits identified earlier have been corrected.

An additional set of criteria against which to judge the strength of a nonprofit organization's possible mission statements include determining whether the statement accomplishes the following:

✔ Does it powerfully articulate the "end" achievement of the organization?

✔ Does it provide criteria for evaluating the success of the organization?

✔ Does it address compelling community needs?

✔ Does it stimulate a desire to join with the organization?

✔ Does it capture the special interests and values of the organization?

✔ Does it differentiate the organization from other organizations?

✔ Does it provide boundaries or focus for the organization?

✔ Does it articulate the organization's "added value" in the community?

Mission statements are discarded and gain support as they are discussed, examined against various criteria, and then discussed some more. One cannot underestimate the amount of time or length of discussion needed when revising a nonprofit organization's mission. Oftentimes, the process appears circular, and there is an iterative nature to the repeated questioning and requestioning of statements, beliefs, and ideals. The mission statement, however, is at the heart of the nonprofit organization, and deserves this demanding exploration.

WHAT IS A VISION?

A vision, on the other hand, offers a fairly detailed scenario of what the organization's ideal should be [Kaufman 1992]. Unlike the mission statement that asks the question, "Why are we here?" the vision is future oriented and answers the question, "What should we be?" An example of a child welfare agency vision might be: "Agency X will be known throughout the state as having the highest quality foster homes."

The organization's strategic business plan may be viewed as the link or road map from the agency's mission to its vision [Jablonski 1992]. The vision is also an ideal that the organization strives for in its efforts to continuously improve both the effectiveness of its internal operations and client programs and services.

Process for Developing a Vision Statement

Visions for organizations often grow out of brainstorming sessions held by the group of individuals charged with developing the vision. Often the agencywide vision is developed by the organization's management team, while visions for other areas of the organization— i.e., lines of business—may be developed by managers and staff members involved in service delivery for that particular area.

The group's brainstorming session may begin with the question, "What do you want the organization to be doing and known for three to five years from now?" Participants then individually respond to the question. The visions should be stated in terms of an ends or outcome, rather than as a means or process. Examples of possible responses may be, "Three to five years from now, the organization will be known as the largest provider (75% market share) of respite care for the state's foster families." And, "Three to five years from now, the organization will be recognized as having one of the best quality assurance programs in the country."

The individual vision statements may then be posted around the meeting room for all participants to review and discuss. As with the development of the mission statement, there are often criteria against which to measure the acceptability of the statement:

✔ Is it a future-oriented statement?

✔ Does it answer the question of what we should be doing and known for three to five years from now?

✔ Does the vision contain enough detail to be meaningful to the organization and others who will read this statement?

✔ Is the statement inspirational?

✔ Will the statement encourage staff to strive to continuously improve the organization?

✔ Is the vision stated in terms of an ends or outcome?

Themes will also emerge as the statements are assessed against the criteria. The statements, or aspects of proposed vision statements, may be grouped into categories. The importance of each of these categories may then be discussed and incorporated into a complete and representative vision statement.

As was the case with the development of the mission statement, proposed visions will be revised repeatedly as they are reviewed against various criteria. While the process may be a draining experience, the vision is an important building block in the development of the organization's strategic business plan. The final vision statement should express sentiments that are shared by all participants.

Mission Development

The Village for Families & Children

As described earlier, the Village for Families & Children has been in existence since 1809. Over the years, the mission of the agency has changed as society and needed services changed. From its early beginnings as an orphanage to its current existence as a multiservice mental health and social services agency, the mission of the agency has evolved. It would be a rare organization that has continued to have the same mission statement over any significant length of time.

Thus, it was not surprising, given the many changes in the environment both outside and inside the agency, that a revised mission statement would be needed. The Village did, in fact, adopt a new mission statement in 1993, when the following three key deficits or motivating forces in revising the mission were identified:

✔ Board members, potential donors, and collaborators had difficulty understanding what the agency did and what it was all about;

✔ The mission was too broad, rather than more focused, to accurately describe the agency; and

✔ Changes in the agency were not reflected in the mission.

The Village's Combined Leadership Team (CLT) members individually drafted mission statements as they answered the question, "Why are we (this organization) here?" Managers then shared their responses with the other team members and the team discussed the pros and cons of each mission draft. The drafts were also tested against the criteria described on page 35. The team took care to assure that any new mission statement addressed the three key deficits. The leadership drafted a mission statement that captured the team's shared sentiments. A small group then "wordsmithed" the statement, modified some of the language, and presented it to the leadership team for a final review and approval.

The statement was then presented to the Board Strategic Planning and Evaluation Committee and Board Executive Committee for their reactions and approval. Ultimately, the full Board of Directors reviewed and approved the new mission statement. The following mission statement became an important foundation during the strategic business plan development:

Our Mission: To reverse the increase in child abuse and violence affecting families in this generation.

The Village for Families & Children

Vision Development

While agency leadership had developed visions in the past, the current strategic business plan expanded the use of visioning to include an agencywide vision, vision statements for each line of business, and such value-added services as research and training. The agency vision was developed by the CLT, while visions for the lines of business and value-added services were developed by work teams associated with those areas.

This description of the Village experience needs to be followed up with a few remarks. The organization's strategic business plan is an internal document that is not usually shared with other organizations or individuals. Thus, the wording of the vision needs to be understood by its intended audience, the organization. There should be little regard for how wording might be perceived or interpreted were it to be used in communicating to various other stakeholders, such as funders or affiliate organizations. A reworded statement that conveys the same meaning is used in instances where such an external communication is required.

The vision for the organization grew out of brainstorming sessions held by the CLT, which was reminded that the visions should be stated in terms of an ends or outcome, rather than as a means or process. The following is an example of a possible statement that would not be acceptable because it pertained to a means: "The Village will employ 500 case workers by 1998." Alternatively, the CLT was told that it would be acceptable to include a vision statement that related to the ends, such as: "The Village will be the predominant provider of case management services for Hartford's AFDC families (60% of families)."

With that initial instruction, CLT members then individually responded to the question, "What do you want the Village to be doing and known for three to five years from now?" To stimulate ideas, examples of possible responses were provided, such as, "Three to five years from now, the Village will be known as the largest provider (75% market share) of respite care for Connecticut's foster families." And "Three to five years from now, the Village will be recognized as having one of the best quality assurance programs in the country." The individual CLT vision statements were then posted around the meeting room for all participants to review; several themes emerged and statements were grouped into the following categories:

- ✔ Role in development of systems of care (e.g., will be known in the state as having the most comprehensive continuum of care for children and families and as the best resource for culturally competent services for African American and Puerto Rican families).

✔ Transitioning with managed care systems (e.g., have at least 80% of the Medicaid Managed Care outpatient to partial hospitalization business in Greater Hartford).

✔ Fiscal stability (e.g., have a highly diversified revenue base, without excessive dependence on any one source).

✔ Adherence to best practices (e.g., in the Hartford area, the Village will be known to have the most effective comprehensive quality assurance and utilization review processes and the quickest response to service requests),

✔ Shift from rehabilitation to resiliency building (e.g., for developing/providing an integrated system of care for seriously emotionally disturbed children that promotes their connectedness to families and communities).

✔ Specific service identifications (e.g., will establish neighborhood-based services in each of the five neighborhood clusters in Hartford).

✔ Positive workplace environment (e.g., will be the first choice of an employer by 80% of Village staff).

The statements were also grouped into agencywide visions and specific line of business or product visions. An example of an agencywide vision was, "The Village will be a major hub in the prevention and rehabilitation system of care for children who have been abused and neglected or suffer from childhood mental, emotional, or behavioral problems." An example of a possible specific line of business or product vision was, "The Village will triple the size of its Workplace Services (employee assistance program) in the state and double its size in the New England region." The latter types of statements, which were specific to a line of business or product, were set aside for future visioning pertaining to that particular line of business.

Subsequent discussion and multiple revisions led to consensus on adopting the following agency vision statement.

Our Vision: The Village for Families & Children, Inc., is the preeminent leader and innovator in promoting healing and growth among children and families in New England.

The Village for Families & Children, Inc., is recognized by the community as the premiere resource and advocate for children and their families.

The Village for Families & Children, Inc., is recognized by its staff for its effectiveness, continuous improvement, cultural diversity and competency, and leadership.

The Village for Families & Children, Inc., is recognized nationally as a center of excellence in innovative program development, applied research, and superior training programs.

As will be described in Chapter 4, work teams in each of the lines of business went through a similar process to develop their own vision statements. All of the line of business visions supported the overall agency vision. Because the agency was applying TQM principles, it was important that consensus be reached regarding the vision. After much discussion, consensus was in fact reached, ensuring to the greatest extent possible that participants were on the same wavelength.

The vision statements were important during many aspects of the strategic business planning process and were touchstones during any key decision making. For example, during strategy selection, one criterion that the potential strategy was assessed by was whether it would forward the vision.

The mission and visions were the anchors of the agency's plan, and their influence will be seen throughout the remainder of the process described in this book.

REFERENCES

Bryson, J. M. (1995). *Strategic planning for public and nonprofit or-ganizations: A guide to strengthening and sustaining organiza-tional achievement.* San Francisco: Jossey-Bass Publishers.

Falsey, T. A. (1989). *Corporate philosophies and mission statements: A survey and guide for corporate communicators and manage-ment.* New York: Quorum.

Jablonski, J. R. (1992). *Implementing TQM: Competing in the nineties through total quality management.* San Diego: Pfeiffer & Com-pany.

Kaufman, R. (1992). *Strategic planning plus: An organizational guide.* Newbury Park, CA: Sage Publications.

Kluger, M. P., & Baker, W. A. (1994). *Innovative leadership in the nonprofit organization: Strategies for change.* Washington, DC: Child Welfare League of America.

Oster, S. M. (1995). *Strategic management for nonprofit organiza-tions: Theory and cases.* New York: Oxford University Press, Inc.

4 Describing a Line of Business

Chapter 2 described the characteristics of the Intensive Children's Services line of business (see page 17). Lines of business are one way of organizing service products that naturally go together, due to their distinct markets and customers. Key criteria for grouping services include the intensity of level of care, source of funding, and type of staffing.

In general, the line of business is described with a few brief paragraphs that are easily understood by any interested party. Typical elements of the description include the following:

✔ The line of business vision statement;

✔ An overall, as well as individual, summary of the programs or services within the line; and

✔ The current market area served.

The vision, programmatic summary, and market area definition developed for a line of business are crafted by individuals familiar with that area of the organization. Line staff and leaders with responsibility for that line of business should be involved, forming a team or line of business work group. In general, the business line description should have the following characteristics:

✔ It should be "short and sweet."

✔ It should identify areas of overlap with other lines of business (e.g., two lines serve the same population, but in different ways).

✔ It should describe the competitive strengths of the line in relation to other area providers.

✔ It should include the line's scope of services.

✔ It should include historical performance (e.g., whether the line has grown within the past three years).

The following sections will discuss each of the three typical elements of the line of business description in greater detail.

THE LINE OF BUSINESS VISION STATEMENT

As stated in Chapter 3, a vision offers a fairly detailed scenario of what the ideal should be [Kaufman 1992]. In terms of the line of business, the vision answers the question, "What should this line of business be?"

Process for Developing a Line of Business Vision Statement

The process described for developing an agencywide vision statement may also be applied in the development of a line of business vision statement. The vision for the line of business may grow out of brainstorming sessions held by the work group or group of line staff and leadership associated with that line of business. As with the organization's vision, the line of business vision is stated in terms of an ends/outcome, not a means/process. An example of a possible statement that would not be acceptable because it pertains to a means would be: "The Intensive Children's Services Line of Business will dedicate three workers to developing new foster homes." Alternatively, it would be acceptable to include a vision statement that pertains to the ends: "The Intensive Children's Services Line of Business will be the predominant provider of specialized foster care homes for the state of Connecticut (75% of families)."

Work group members in each line of business may individually respond to the question, "What do you want the line of business to be doing and known for three to five years from now?" Examples of possible responses may be given: "Three to five years from now, the Intensive Children's Services Line of Business will be known as the largest provider (80% market share) of extended day treatment services for Connecticut's adolescent population." And "Three to five years from now, the Intensive Children's Services Line of Business will be recognized as having a leading comprehensive system of care."

Previous statements that may have been identified during the agencywide visioning, which were actually specific to a line of business, may also be reviewed at this time. A draft of a line of business vision statement is then shared with members of the organization's other lines of business. This is an opportunity for questions to be asked, clarifications made, and any overlaps identified and addressed.

SUMMARY OF THE LINE OF BUSINESS PROGRAMS

The services and programs within a line of business are the tools with which to strive toward realizing the line's vision. The program summary should emphasize the commonalities across the various services, as well as indicate places where there are differences.

Services within a line of business, for example, may be a mix of nonprofit and for-profit services. Often, the for-profit ventures serve as a source of revenue to fund nonprofit endeavors. This strategy is referred to as nonprofit venturing [Skloot 1987]. Thus, while the source of funding is often a factor in grouping services or products into lines of business, extenuating circumstances—such as a desire to diversify funding and varying financial expectations—make it possible for programs within the line of business to have different funders.

In addition to the services or programs within a line of business, the program summary may also include values held by the line. For example, cultural diversity may be of particular importance to a line of business and be a consideration that runs throughout the strategic planning process. Another value that may be important is TQM or continuous quality improvement [Jablonski 1992]. Ways in which

TQM has and could be incorporated into services may also be highlighted in the summary, if it is of particular value to the organization.

Process for Developing a Summary of the Line of Business Programs

A first step in developing the line of business program summary is to hold a brainstorming session where individual descriptors or characteristics of the line of business are identified.

Commonalities across the programs or services within the line of business will become apparent, as well as traits that distinguish this group of services from another group of services. A large list may be reduced through discussion and/or a rank-ordering process. For example, participants in a line of business work group may individually vote for the five characteristics they think are most relevant to furthering understanding of the line of business. Those characteristics that receive the most votes can then be included in the final summary. The summary is then reviewed by the larger planning group to assure that the material is clear to others outside the line of business.

THE LINE OF BUSINESS MARKET AREA

One question to wrestle with in strategic planning is, "How wide is the population that the organization wants to serve?" This question could range from a discussion of the geographic extent of the market area to the age of the clients to be served.

A line of business may have primary as well as secondary market areas. For example, the majority of families may come from one particular area; however, there may also be a significant minority that resides in another area. A strategy may be developed to cultivate a secondary market. An alternative strategy may be to reduce a secondary market, while maintaining and building a concentration in the primary market area.

Another factor to consider with regard to a line of business market area is that the services or products within a line may have many characteristics in common, but still serve families from varied areas. The differences that distinguish these services need to be identified. If the description of the market area, however, is so broad as to include all agency products, then the information is not specific enough to aid in later planning.

Market area information may be presented in the form of a table, pie chart, or map. As the information is gathered for each of the organization's lines of business, a contrast of the market areas across lines can be useful. A comparison helps to highlight the similarities and differences and assists in office location planning and agencywide transportation issues.

Process for Determining a Line of Business Market Area

At the very least, the market area definition should begin with a description of where the current clients reside geographically. This information may be based on client ZIP code or street address. The market area or residence of current clients served is ideally defined through plotting or summarizing the locations from addresses. Many of the larger organizations, or agencies within a network, have automated information systems. These management information systems will most likely contain the clients' street address and town.

In addition to plotting the information on a map, the data can also be presented as the percentage of clients who live in urban, suburban, or rural areas, or by region or county. If all the clients are from an urban area, sections of a city can be further delineated by ZIP code or telephone exchanges. For an organization that serves clients from only suburban or only rural areas, regions or towns may be segmented in an effort to come up with a meaningful way to describe the population served. This information may be useful in later strategy planning, for example, to pinpoint areas that may be currently underserved, where a new office might be opened, or transportation provided to the most heavily client-saturated areas.

In the case of foster care and other child placement programs, both the address of the biological family, as well as the placement location, may be useful in planning. Pinpointing the location of the biological homes may be helpful, for example, in developing foster homes in those areas. This may remove what could otherwise be a barrier to visitation of foster children by their biological families. It could also reduce the likelihood of having a child change schools and disrupt other activities and community supports.

The Village for Families & Children As stated in Chapter 2, the Village identified four lines of business during its recent strategic business planning process. The Intensive Children's Services line of business will be shared as an example for other child welfare organizations to consult when developing their own strategic business plans.

The vision statement for the Intensive Children's Services (ICS) was developed by a work group consisting of eight agency members. Participants included program staff, managers overseeing these programs, the agency's President, and the Grants Officer. The agency's chief planner (and coauthor of this book), was a member of each line of business work group and occasionally attended portions of meetings to assist with the process.

The ICS work group followed the process just described. They held a brainstorming session where members were asked to think of ends- or outcomes-type statements. Work group members individually responded to the question, "What do you want the line of business to be doing and known for three to five years from now?"

Using flipchart paper, members then shared individual vision statements. Previous statements identified during the agencywide visioning that were actually specific to the ICS line of business were also added to the list. During group discussion, themes emerged and statements were grouped into categories.

A draft of the vision statement was developed and shared with members of the organization's other lines of business. Members clarified questions and addressed overlaps with other lines of business. The following ICS vision statement resulted from this process:

The Village for Families & Children will be the premier private provider safeguarding and healing the region's highest risk children.

Toward this end, Intensive Children's Services will be widely recognized as

- an effective developer of self-sufficiency in children and families,

- a leading comprehensive system/continuum of care,

- a leading developer of culturally competent therapeutic services, and

- a leading advocate for children and families.

After the vision statement was developed, the ICS line of business description was then addressed. This process began with a review of the seven programs currently within the ICS line. From a brainstorming session, members developed a list of common themes, philosophies, and descriptors. Traits that distinguished ICS from the other lines of business were included in the list. The list was then narrowed through a rank-ordering process.

The work group developed a general line of business descriptor based on these traits and wrote the specific descriptions of each of the seven programs within the line. Two values were especially important to the Intensive Children's Services line of business: the value of cultural competency and the capabilities of staff.

The formal ICS line of business description is as follows:

The Village for Families & Children, Inc., Intensive Services for Children provides family and community-based services for children and families who have experienced or are at risk of abuse, neglect, and family disruption.

Services include comprehensive assessment, treatment, case management, family preparation, and child placement, guided by a unified philosophy of care that emphasizes collaboration and coordination. Services are flexible to meet 24-hour, 7-days-per-week care needs.

Qualified professional, paraprofessional, and lay staff provide culturally competent services that meet or exceed national standards of care.

The Intensive Children's Services line of business consists of the following programs:

- ✔ **Extended Day Treatment:** A comprehensive clinical treatment service provided to children who exhibit emotional and behavioral problems to stabilize and improve their adaptive functioning, thereby decreasing the risk of out-of-home or community placement.

- ✔ **Specialized Foster Care:** Meeting clinical and permanency needs through professional treatment foster care and providing a normalizing family life with comprehensive, individualized case planning service and collaboration.

- ✔ **Treatment Choice:** Similar to Specialized Foster Care except for restriction of one child per foster home because of severity of child's needs.

- ✔ **Wraparound Service:** Provides highly individualized flexible services to sustain children in families and communities (most often accomplished through the use of child/youth mentors).

- ✔ **Intensive Family Preservation:** An intensive, time-limited, home-based program that provides support and therapeutic services to Hartford families with at least one child at imminent risk of placement outside their home.

- ✔ **Family Reunification:** Provides parent and child interventions and visitation leading to optimal level of family reconnectedness.

✔ **Special Needs Adoption:** Provides permanent placement for special needs children in adoptive homes to interrupt the cycle of abuse, violence, and neglect.

Following development of the ICS program description, the work group then addressed the market area definition, which posed particular challenges for the Intensive Children's Services line of business. The current area served was first determined from the agency's annual client profile and automated information on client addresses. The percentage of clients residing in a particular geographic area of the city and surrounding suburbs was calculated, based on ZIP codes. An added twist for this line of business was that a foster parent address, for example, was not necessarily in the same area as that of a biological parent. Which address should be used? The issue was resolved by providing the work group with both pieces of information, including an extra summary table containing a breakout for the biological parent addresses. This latter piece of information, while not included in the final market area definition, was used in subsequent strategy development for the ICS line.

Another complicating factor was that the market area could not be described in an overall fashion, as it differed by service within the line of business. Further, the public child protective agency serves the state according to regions and expects its private contractors to offer service to an entire region. This information then, was factored into the following market area description:

> The market area for Intensive Children's Services varies by product and was defined on the basis of the town of residence of children and foster families served, and the relative geographic market position of the Village.

> The primary service areas were defined to include DCF (the state child welfare agency) Regions IV and VI—encompassing the Greater Hartford area and extending north to the Massachusetts border and east to the Rhode Island border.

Secondarily, because the ICS of the Village is considered to be a statewide resource, the remaining areas of the state (outside of the primary service area) are considered to be a secondary market area for the ICS business line.

The strategic business plan report contained a state map with primary and secondary market areas shaded accordingly. The report also contained an appendix with detailed information comparing client residence for each of the lines of business.

The description of the ICS line of business was shared with the full planning group. Suggestions were offered and modifications made accordingly.

REFERENCES

Jablonski, J. R. (1992). *Implementing TQM: Competing in the nineties through total quality management.* San Diego: Pfeiffer & Company.

Kaufman, R. (1992). *Strategic planning plus: An organizational guide.* Newbury Park, CA: Sage Publications.

Skloot, E. (1987). Enterprise and commerce in nonprofit organizations. In W. W. Powell (Ed.), *The nonprofit sector: A research handbook*, New Haven, CT: Yale University Press.

5 Leading a Situational Assessment

A thorough and frank examination of the organization is an important aspect of any strategic business plan. A situational assessment is one tool to use to examine the organization's services, current populations served, strengths and weaknesses, and funding sources [Kluger & Baker 1994]. This examination provides information necessary for an analysis of the organization's Strengths, Weaknesses, Opportunities, and Threats—otherwise known as a SWOT Analysis. The SWOT Analysis is an important part of the well-known and respected Harvard Policy Model of strategic planning [Barry 1986] and assures that internal strengths and weaknesses of an organization are assessed in relation to the external opportunities and threats in the environment. In general, strengths and weaknesses relate more to the present, while opportunities and threats are more often associated with the future [Nutt & Backoff 1992]. The strengths and weaknesses thus lend themselves to an inward examination, while the opportunities and threats may best be assessed by turning outward. (Chapter 6 describes the external assessment.)

A Threats-Opportunities-Weaknesses-Strengths matrix, or TOWS Matrix [Weihrich 1982] suggests that there are four types of strategies that may be developed from this kind of analysis:

✔ **SO Strategies** employ strengths to take advantage of identified opportunities,

✔ **WO Strategies** attempt to overcome weaknesses by taking advantage of opportunities available to the organization,

✔ **ST Strategies** employ strengths to avoid threats, and

✔ **WT Strategies** defensively reduce weaknesses as well as avoid threats.

An examination of the agency's strengths will also lead to an understanding of the organization's "core competencies" [Prahalad & Hamel 1990] or "capabilities" [Stalk et al. 1992]. These competencies or capabilities may be drawn upon throughout strategy development and implementation. The organization's strengths and advantages over the competition have also been referred to as "strategic competencies" [Shanklin & Ryans 1985].

GATHERING INFORMATION

Information for the situational assessment is collected from multiple sources, with each providing a different perspective. Typical sources include program staff, clients, and representatives from organizations that refer clients to the agency. Information from each of these sources may be collected in various ways.

One way to collect information is through a **program staff self-assessment survey**. As its name implies, a self-assessment survey is completed by the staff who provide service for that particular program. Survey questions may elicit a description of the service, organization, and staff; funding and costs; benefits and shortfalls; and strengths of the competition.

Once the self-assessment surveys are completed, a chart comparing responses to key questions by services within a line of business may be developed. By showing responses to questions side by side, obvious similarities, as well as differences, emerge. These differences and similarities will be factored into the resulting strategies for furthering the line of business.

Similarly, strengths and weaknesses will also be identified and incorporated into the development of strategies. During deliberations of which strategies to select, consideration should be given, for example, to expanding the strong areas of the organization. Building on strengths and addressing weaknesses will help the overall health of the agency, as well as the quality of the resulting strategic business plan.

In addition to program staff answering questions on the self-assessment survey, data may be obtained from the organization's **management information system**. The MIS data may include demographic information on the various populations served, such as the clients' gender, age, income, and marital status. Because strategic business planning is based on actual data, it is expected that this source of information will be especially useful as strategies are developed and debated.

Another source of information for the situational assessment is the **client**. In this era of making every effort to satisfy clients and be client driven, this perspective is an important part of planning for the future. Interviewing clients is one way to gather this information. Another way is through a client questionnaire. If the agency has a client satisfaction survey, for example, then relevant questions might be added or substituted during the time such information is needed. Clients can be most helpful in suggesting service improvements, as well as identifying what they perceive as strengths or advantages of the organization and its services. As noted by Mika [1996], however, one should be cautious in using such measures for populations with low literacy levels.

Collecting information from representatives of **referring organizations** is yet another source for the situational assessment. In addition to gathering information from program staff and clients, it is also important to understand what personnel from referring organizations think about the agency. For child welfare agencies, these organizations most likely include the state's department for children and families or child protective services. Use of a structured focus group format is an ideal way to gather information simultaneously from a group of referring organizations. The authors recommend use of the nominal group technique, a method pioneered by Delbecq et al. [1975].

The nominal group technique is a method that allows equal participation and weighting in obtaining group opinion. Participants individually respond to a question posed by the facilitator and through a round-robin process, all ideas are recorded on a flipchart. A voting process then determines the items given the highest priority by the participants. Refer to Moore [1987] for a detailed, step-by-step description of the nominal group technique.

In the case of the situational assessment, questions asked of participants might include what they think are the strengths and weaknesses of the programs they refer to and in what ways the programs could be improved.

The Village for Families & Children The Village has conducted situational assessments for many years. The first self-assessment survey was developed by questions solicited from Village staff [Kluger & Baker 1994]. The service self-assessment survey was completed through staff member responses and information from the agency's management information system. Clients, as well as representatives from organizations that refer clients to the Village, also provided information for the Village's situational assessment. The following sections describes each of these sources of information and the way in which data were collected.

The Program Staff's Self-Assessment Survey

A thorough examination of each existing service was done through program staff response to a series of approximately 30 questions. (Please see Appendix A for a complete copy of the questions.) The topics included the following:

- ✔ Service description (e.g., "What types of services and treatment modalities are offered?");

- ✔ Description of service organization and staff (e.g., "How many staff does your service have, and what are their roles?");

✔ Service funding and costs (e.g., "How are fees for clients determined and communicated?");

✔ Clients/consumers (e.g., "How would you characterize your markets?");

✔ Product benefits/shortfalls (e.g., "Why do our clients come to us for service?"); and

✔ Competition (e.g., "What do your competitors do better than you?").

Staff were asked to identify product benefits and shortfalls from client, staff, and funder perspectives. Cultural competency and service effectiveness were also part of the assessment.

Competition was an area that had been examined superficially during previous strategic planning at the Village. The current situational assessment also included questions about what agency staff thought competitors did better than the Village. As will be described in Chapter 7, the current strategic business planning process also included the collection of information directly from competitors.

Tables comparing responses to key questions by services within a line of business were prepared. For example, the table for the Intensive Children's Services line of business listed the questions and had columns containing the responses from each of the programs in that line of business, such as foster care, adoption, and extended day treatment. By showing responses to questions side by side, obvious similarities and differences could be detected. These differences and similarities were factored into the resulting strategic business plan as strategies for furthering the line of business as a whole were developed.

An outcome of the self-assessment survey was that strengths and weaknesses were also identified and incorporated into the development of strategies. During deliberations of which strategies to select, for example, consideration was given to expanding the strong areas of the organization.

An excerpt from the table for Intensive Children's Services is shown in Appendix B. To summarize, the following strengths and weaknesses were identified from the self-assessment survey:

ICS Strengths

✔ The cultural diversity and cultural competency of staff;

✔ The comprehensiveness/scope of services provided (multiple treatment modalities);

✔ The coordination of services along the continuum, within the line of business, and with other lines of business;

✔ Enhanced quality and efficiency of care through a multidisciplined team approach;

✔ Comprehensive case management;

✔ Accredited, licensed;

✔ Endowment available for new initiatives;

✔ Grantsmanship and collaboration with community organizations;

✔ Not a "Johnny Come Lately"—have a rich history, stability in providing child welfare services;

✔ Training program;

✔ Ever-increasing demands for service;

✔ Strong from a fundraising, funder perspective; and

✔ Good work and service location.

ICS Weaknesses

✔ Dependence on state child welfare agency as principal funder,

✔ Dependence on endowment as a significant funder,

✔ A need for more bilingual clinical staff and African American male staff, and

✔ Limited capacity to meet the demand for services.

Information that described the various populations served was gathered wherever possible from the agency's automated management information system. Strategic business planning workgroups were provided with demographic information on agency services, such as the clients' gender, age, income, and marital status.

Client Interviews

As mentioned earlier, the client perspective is an important part of planning for the future. Thus, it was fortuitous that, coincidental to the development of the strategic business plan, testing of a client satisfaction survey was also occurring. The Village took advantage of this opportunity to collect client information useful to the development of the strategic business plan.

Interviews were conducted as clients waited in the reception area prior to their outpatient mental health service appointments. After agreeing to complete the survey, an interviewer asked nine of the clients to answer written questions rating their satisfaction with aspects of the service they received. The survey also had two open-ended questions that asked what was most helpful and what could be done to make the clients' experience at the Village a better one.

Following completion of the survey, clients were interviewed by a research assistant about the clarity of the questions. The research assistant also questioned the clients about why they had chosen the Village for services and what changes they would like to see made at the Village. All responses were recorded on paper and then summarized by the chief planner. Comments on what was most helpful related to satisfaction with their service providers, including having someone to talk to whom they could trust, and who would provide constant support and dedication.

With regard to what could be done to make their Village experiences better, two specific suggestions were "a group for kids with the same problems" and "better availability of psychiatrist." Clients also gave reasons for why they chose the Village, which often related to the quality of the service:

✔ Impressed by intake and initial phone contact;

✔ Always a phone number to call when worker isn't in;

✔ Feeling of not being shuffled around, worker really cared; and

✔ Heard it was good—similar program in suburb where client lives, but that program has a bad reputation.

Others chose the Village by looking in the telephone book, were referred by a social worker or other person, or because the Village was accepted by the client's insurance. Clients suggested the following changes:

✔ Village newsletter for clients;

✔ Accessible, off-hours telephone service (person answering invades privacy of client);

✔ Bills that are easier for less educated people to read;

✔ Snack machines in the Welcome Center;

✔ More updated magazines in the Welcome Center;

✔ Better availability of psychiatrist;

✔ Have a group for children with similar problems;

✔ Have same counselor during the course of treatment (son sees too many different counselors and gets attached to them before they leave);

✔ Have more male counselors; and

✔ Have a better playground with more activities.

Focus Group with Representatives from Referring Organizations

As discussed earlier, it is useful to understand what personnel from referring organizations think about the agency. Additional information was collected through interviews with personnel from referring organizations during the competitive analysis (see Chapter 7). The intent of the data collection, however, was different in the two contacts and did not include the same personnel.

In the current strategic business planning, the Managed Behavioral Health Services line of business thought it would be helpful to know what personnel from referring organizations thought about their services. To gather that information, a focus group was held for representatives from agencies that make referrals to the Village's managed behavioral health services. A total of 14 people participated from such organizations as the state's department of social services, hospital pediatric intensive care units, police departments, and the local urban league.

The focus group was conducted by Miriam Kluger using the nominal group technique described earlier. There were five questions posed to the group:

✔ What do you think are the strengths of our Outpatient Services and Trauma Service?

✔ If you had the choice, would you refer to a private group or the Village? Why?

✔ What do you think are the weaknesses of our Outpatient Services and Trauma Service?

✔ How could we improve our services and/or overcome our weaknesses?

✔ What kind of feedback do you receive from families that you refer to us?

In general, referring agencies in attendance thought that the Village had the following positive attributes:

✔ It provided high-quality services ("one of the best providers of high-quality child therapy in Connecticut");

✔ It is well known in the community, especially Clark Clinic ("the Village is a household word in the community"); and

✔ It is comfortable and welcoming to clients because of its culturally diverse staff and safe, convenient location.

Suggested Improvements

✔ Improve the process for referring to the Village,

✔ Regularly provide information about the Village services and referral process to referring organizations,

✔ Improve timeliness of interagency collaborations,

✔ Extend hours to evenings and Saturdays,

✔ Expand the Weaver High School program to other high schools and middle schools, and

✔ Become more connected to such basic need services as food and shelter.

In summary, the situational assessment examined the organization in a detailed manner from several perspectives. During the course of the planning, this information was part of a report that was consulted during selection of strategies and as information that remained in the back of the planners' minds.

REFERENCES

Barry, B. W. (1986). *Strategic planning workbook for nonprofit organizations.* St. Paul, MN: Amherst H. Wilder Foundation.

Delbecq, A. L., Van de Ven, A. H., & Gustafson, D. H. (1975). *Group techniques for program planning: A guide to nominal group and delphi processes.* Glenview, IL: Scott-Foresman.

Kluger, M. K., & Baker, W. A. (1994). *Innovative leadership in the nonprofit organization: Strategies for change.* Washington DC: Child Welfare League of America.

Mika, K. L. (1996). *Program outcome evaluation: A step-by-step handbook.* Milwaukee, WI: Families International, Inc.

Moore, C. (1987). *Group techniques for idea building.* Newbury Park, CA: Sage Publications.

Nutt, P. C., & Backoff, R. W. (1992). *Strategic management for public and third sector organizations: A handbook for leaders.* San Francisco: Jossey-Bass.

Prahalad, C. K., & Hamel, G. (1990, May/June). The core competence of the corporation. *Harvard Business Review, 68*(3), 79-91.

Shanklin, W. L., & Ryans, J. K., Jr. (1985). *Thinking strategically: Planning for your company's future.* New York: Random House, Inc.

Stalk, G., Evans, P., & Shulman, L. E. (1992, March/April). Competing on capabilities: The new rules of corporate strategy. *Harvard Business Review, 70*(2), 57-69.

Weihrich, H. (1982). The TOWS matrix: A tool for situational analysis. *Long Range Planning, 15* (2), 61.

6 Conducting an External Assessment

A key ingredient for success in leading a nonprofit organization is being able to anticipate trends and prepare for change [Rosenberg 1992]. The community the organization serves is not static, and new challenges or needs emerge over time [Kluger & Baker 1994].

One way to monitor these emerging trends or needs is to conduct an external assessment. Also referred to as an environmental scan, the external assessment is an important aspect of strategic business planning. It identifies future trends, problems, or issues that may become opportunities or threats to the agency. (This is the second part of the SWOT analysis mentioned in Chapter 5.) The list of opportunities and threats should be finite and center on identifying key variables that will lead to actions on the part of the organization [David 1993]. These actions may be offensive or defensive responses that take advantage of external opportunities and reduce the effect of possible threats.

This chapter describes how to conduct an external assessment and provides examples of major trends in health and child welfare that were important to the strategic business planning which occurred at the Village.

HOW TO CONDUCT AN EXTERNAL ASSESSMENT

The external assessment identifies national, regional, and local trends that may impact the organization. Trends are sometimes classified as social, economic, political, and technological. Child welfare and other nonprofit organizations may be affected by trends in all of these categories. For example, such social trends as shifts in minority population, teen pregnancy rates, and child abuse and neglect rates, are all of relevance to child welfare agencies. Economic trends, such as poverty rates, the affordability and adequacy of housing, and homelessness rates also have implications for child welfare and other nonprofit agencies. Even political trends, such as changes in elected officials and commissioners, can result in congressional votes that have significant ramifications for funding programs that are particularly important to the organization and the community it serves.

National trends are often captured in reports produced by major national nonprofit organizations. Examples of such organizations are the United Way and Family Service America. These reports are regularly sent to members or are available to nonmembers for a modest fee. Professional journals and national association newsletters and conferences may also prove useful in obtaining information on national trends.

Information on state and local trends may be collected from printed material, such as state or local government reports and newspapers. Information may also be found through local chambers of commerce and local or regional polling centers.

Data on trends that are more narrow in scope, but impact the agency and community directly, may also be gathered through structured focus groups with key stakeholders. The authors again recommend use of the nominal group technique, a method pioneered by Delbecq and Van de Ven [Delbecq et al. 1975]. The nominal group technique is a method that allows equal participation and weighting in obtaining group opinion. Participants individually respond to a question posed by the facilitator, and through a round-robin process, all ideas are recorded on a flipchart.

In the current application, the focus group question might ask participants to identify the most crucial trends, problems, or issues facing the community that the organization serves. Participants then offer their opinions during this brainstorming aspect of the process with the assurance that reactions or debate of ideas are not permitted. Once all stakeholders are clear on what each item means, then a confidential vote is taken with participants selecting the five trends (or three trends, depending on the number of trends identified by participants) that they believe are most important. The items may then be rank ordered by the number of votes received. The resulting list identifies the major trends, problems, and issues as viewed by the more immediate community within which the organization exists. [See Moore 1987 for a step-by-step, detailed description of nominal group technique.]

In addition to focus groups, sources of information for the external assessment may include the organization's leaders and program staff members. A consultant may also be helpful in gathering information for the external assessment, particularly if the consultant is an expert in an area of immediate importance to the organization. Regardless of who obtains the information, the external assessment is a necessary component of the strategic business planning process.

The Village for Families & Children The Village gathered information from several sources for the external assessment aspect of the strategic business planning process. The consultant engaged to assist in the strategic planning was also quite knowledgeable about managed care. He gave a written and oral presentation to the full planning group on the topic. The President of the Village also reported on trends in behavioral health, child welfare, and systems of care. Relevant articles were shared, as well as reports from national organizations. Because many readers will find these trends relevant to their settings, the following section provides an overview of the major trends in health and child welfare.

MAJOR TRENDS IN HEALTH AND CHILD WELFARE

The following are examples of major trends in health and child welfare that were important to the strategic business planning which occurred at the authors' agency:

✔ For-profits have entered into Health and Human Services.

✔ The behavioral health care industry is characterized by rapid change in both the delivery and reimbursement of health care.

✔ Historical cost-based incentives created an oversupply of providers, excess inpatient capacity, and tremendous growth in the health care dollars spent on behavioral health services.

✔ Past incentives focused on inpatient care and ignored the efficiencies of other modes of care.

✔ In response to the spiraling growth in costs, "managed behavioral health care organizations" developed:

- utilization management systems,
- cost-control mechanisms, and
- selected panels of providers.

✔ Employers have rapidly shifted to managed behavioral health care organizations (85% of companies with more than 1,000 employees contract with MBHOs; 59.8% of all insured Americans received mental health benefits through some form of managed care).

✔ Child welfare and community social services have been included in the managed care system.

✔ Hospitals and hospital chains are jockeying for market position in child welfare and social services.

✔ Setting of cost and eligibility limits by employers has resulted in cost-shifting to the public sector.

✔ The public sector has also changed in response to managing behavioral health benefits—led by Medicaid reform efforts that have integrated or "blurred" private and public sector programs.

✔ There have been reductions in government revenue.

✔ Provider responses to these changes have included
  - improved management of patient care through stronger and more sophisticated utilization management;
  - vertical (system) integration and horizontal expansion (provider networks);
  - development of financial risk-sharing arrangements;
  - diversification of services and expanded outpatient modes of care; and
  - adding additional benefits for customers (EAP, on-site programs, satellite clinics, etc.).

✔ "Systems of care" development through affiliations, alliances, and acquisitions.

✔ In general, MCOs are seeking behavioral health providers who can add value through
  - low cost;
  - demonstrated high quality;
  - improved outcomes;
  - documented success in utilization management;
  - enhanced access (e.g., geographic coverage and 24-hour coverage); and
  - broad scope of services ("one-stop shopping").

✔ There has been an erosion of traditional geographic and service boundaries.

✔ There is a trend toward empowering parents and neighborhoods.

REFERENCES

David, F. R. (1993). *Strategic management* (4th ed.). New York: Macmillan Publishing Company.

Delbecq, A. L., Van de Ven, A. H., & Gustafson, D. H. (1975). *Group techniques for program planning: A guide to nominal group and delphi processes.* Glenview, IL: Scott-Foresman.

Kluger, M. P., & Baker, W. A. (1994). *Innovative leadership in the nonprofit organization: Strategies for change.* Washington, DC: Child Welfare League of America.

Moore, C. (1987). *Group techniques for idea building.* Newbury Park, CA: Sage Publications.

Rosenberg, D. (1992). Eliminating resistance to change: The magic formula. *Nonprofit World, 10* (5), 33-34.

7 Commissioning a Competitive Analysis

Before an organization can analyze its competition, it must first define the arena or industry that it operates in [Oster 1995]. For example, is the organization in the business of finding foster homes for abused children, or in stemming the increase in child abuse? The definition of the industry or market will influence which competitors are studied. The organization's mission statement is a good resource for determining this market definition.

Once the arena or industry has been defined, then the organization can identify competitors. Management and staff and any others involved in the organization's strategic business planning, such as a consultant, may first develop a list of current competitors by thinking back to the last few times that the organization tried to secure a grant or contract. In instances where the organization was successful in being awarded the grant or contract, what other agencies or organizations also applied for funding? In cases where the organization did not receive funding, what were the organizations that did secure the funding? These names form the basis for the list of current competitors.

In addition to current competitors, there are also new, potential, or emerging competitors. These may be new organizations that are considering providing similar services or products. There may be organizations that have existed for quite some time that are thinking of branching out into the marketplace in which the planning organization competes. There is also the possibility of a for-profit organization expanding into a marketplace that was traditionally served by nonprofit agencies. This is the case, for example, in the foster care arena. These organizations should all be considered competitors and added to the list being developed. As Pearce and Robinson [1994] suggest, one of the common mistakes that organizations make when identifying competitors is overemphasizing present and known competitors and not giving enough attention to potential competitors.

Key funders are another source to consider when conducting a competitive analysis. Key funders may include the state or local government departments that refer clients to the agency, such as the state child welfare or social services departments, and if applicable, the local United Way agency. These entities offer a different perspective on competition. They may help the nonprofit understand, from a funder's point of view, strengths and weaknesses of the organization as stacked up against other organizations.

A discussion of competitive analysis in the nonprofit arena would not be complete without mention of the philosophical shift required for some managers in this field to even begin thinking in this way. Unlike for-profit businesses, leaders of nonprofit organizations have traditionally focused on their missions and placed value on cooperation across agencies [Weiner 1982]. In fact, many funders, including government and private foundations, believe a proposal is stronger if it shows that the applicant is partnering with other nonprofit organizations. Further, the problems and social issues to which these organizations are dedicated are too large to be solved solely by any one entity. By working together, nonprofit organizations with similar missions can strive to attain a common goal that can not be reached by one organization acting alone [Laufer 1984]. However, they are challenged to be both cooperative and competitive as resources shrink and for-profits enter arenas traditionally served by nonprofit agencies. Organizations are partners and collaborators one day and competitors the next day. A new paradigm discussed by Moore [1996] is referred to as "market creation": thinking in terms of the larger picture or environment and how several organizations can join together to shape networks and develop future strategies. There is no easy or obvious solution to this dilemma. Perhaps acknowledgment of this dichotomy will encourage dialogue and ease the discomfort for some of the parties involved.

Once the current and emerging competitors have been identified, then information needs to be collected. Answers to the following three questions will help shape the plan for data collection:

- ✔ What does the organization wish to know about its competitors?

- ✔ What does the organization wish to know from its key funders?

- ✔ How will this information be obtained?

WHAT DOES THE ORGANIZATION WISH TO KNOW ABOUT ITS COMPETITORS?

When examining competitors, we are interested in their strengths and weaknesses, particularly as they relate to areas of opportunity [Mockler 1989]. If, for example, a competitor is especially strong, having tangibly demonstrated its efficacy by securing most of the available contracts in a particular sector, then it would be difficult to break into that area. A weakness, on the other hand, represents an opportunity for a potentially stronger organization to compete head-to-head. A new service or product may also be developed to fill a niche where an unfilled need is present.

Much can also be learned from the deficits or mistakes of the competition. A new service or product can be developed that addresses these weaknesses and builds on the organization's strengths as identified during the situational assessment. Rather than developing a new service, another possibility is that the difficulties that must be overcome to succeed in a particular sector make it unlikely that the organization conducting the competitive analysis will be any more successful than others who have gone before it.

One way to determine what specific questions to ask competitors is to have the planning group brainstorm a list of possible questions (a parallel process may take place in preparation of interviews with key funders). Keep in mind that an organization can acquire a leading market position only if it offers clients a superior product or an improved solution to a problem at a competitive rate [Hinterhuber & Popp 1992]. This understanding will help dictate which questions to include in the competitive analysis.

Once all possible questions have been identified, then similar questions may be grouped into categories. Questions from each category are then selected to assure that all the areas are covered. Wording of questions may then be finalized. Some examples of questions that might be asked of competitors include the following:

✔ How many clients do you see per week/month?

✔ Has your volume increased or decreased over the last three years?

✔ What is the cost for your services?

✔ What geographic area do you generally draw your cases from?

✔ Do you anticipate expanding your geographic coverage?

✔ Who do you consider your chief competitors?

✔ What services/products do you have that you will eliminate/downsize or anticipate difficulties in sustaining?

✔ What new services are you thinking of offering?

WHAT DOES THE ORGANIZATION WISH TO KNOW FROM ITS KEY FUNDERS?

Funders provide a different, but important, perspective regarding the nonprofit and how well it stacks up against the competition, which is often other nonprofits. Information about what the funders view as the agency's strengths and weaknesses of the nonprofit will influence changes and strategies the organization may select, as well as changes in the way funding applications are prepared.

Listed below are some examples of questions that might be asked of key funders:

- ✔ What do you feel are the current gaps in services?

- ✔ Which agencies do you feel are competitive with _____ (name of the organization that commissioned the competitive analysis)?

- ✔ What do you consider to be the strengths of _____ (name of the organization that commissioned the competitive analysis)?

- ✔ What do you consider to be the weaknesses of _____ (name of the organization that commissioned the competitive analysis)?

- ✔ What criteria do you consider important when evaluating organizations for funding?

- ✔ What major concerns do you have for the future?

HOW WILL THIS INFORMATION BE OBTAINED?

The information may be obtained in a variety of ways, and one is not necessarily superior to another. The method chosen will depend on several factors. Is the organization comfortable having staff members ask competitors and funders the questions, or do they prefer a third party, such as a consultant or some other external group? In addition to the "who" being determined, the "how" also needs to be addressed. Telephone or in-person interviews are ideal. Structured focus groups are another technique. The authors discourage the use of mailed surveys, however, because of the usually poor return rate and inability to ask clarifying questions. An alternative is to use a combination of several of these data collection strategies. For example, the agency might first try to arrange a focus group. For those unable to make the focus group, then a second option would be to request a telephone interview.

The organization should establish a timeframe for collecting this information. This process is then repeated periodically, depending upon how quickly the environment is changing. A one- to two-year cycle for conducting a competitive analysis is a realistic timeframe.

The collected information may be organized for later use as a reference in developing new programs or products. The overall conclusions also provide food for thought in developing agencywide strategies. For ease of use, the results of the competitive analysis should be organized by line of business. For example, information from competitors and funders of the organization's child welfare services should be grouped in one section. Suggested resolutions of any differences in perspectives may also be offered in this section.

The Village for Families & Children The Village's competitive analysis began with a discussion among members of the lines of business as to what they truly considered their services and products to be. This was done in preparation for collecting information from current and potential competitors of the Intensive Children's Services and Managed Behavioral Health Services lines of business. The agency chose to focus on these two lines of business because they were felt to have experienced, or were anticipating, the greatest change. Much of the change was driven by managed care companies and the expectation that many of the agency's services within these two lines of business would be required to operate within a managed care environment. In contrast, the Neighborhood and Family Strengthening Services line of business contained many new programs, that, as a part of their development, had examined similar services other organizations were offering. The Workplace Services line of business had considered its competition since its inception and was already aware of other organizations offering similar services.

The Village chose to use a consultant to conduct its competitive analysis. The authors and consultant concurred that the Intensive Children's Services and Managed Behavioral Health Services competitive analyses would serve as a model that the Village's chief planner could then replicate with other lines of business, should the need arise.

There were several reasons why a consultant was asked to conduct the competitive analysis rather than attempt to have agency staff do it. To begin with, this was the first time the agency had authorized a competitive analysis, and the process felt quite foreign to the organization. Second, there was a degree of comfort in having an external party, separate from the Village, conduct the interviews. Third, there was also the consideration that an element of separation could lend objectivity to the effort and an ability to receive the responses in a detached manner.

As noted, this full-scale competitive analysis was in distinct contrast to previous Village strategic planning. In the past, efforts had been made to consider the competition without actually obtaining data directly from the identified organizations. Similarly, interviews with key agency funders of Village programs, including the state child welfare department and the local United Way, had not been conducted on this particular subject.

The work teams for the Intensive Children's Services and Managed Behavioral Health Services lines of business provided the consultant with the names of current and potential competitors. Through a combination of telephone and in-person interviews, as well as gathering of printed information such as brochures, annual reports, and public documents, the organization developed a profile of the competition.

The questions asked during the interviews were determined from suggestions made by the full planning team, work groups associated with the two lines of business, and the consultant. The questions inquired about the competition's strengths and weaknesses, future plans, and what they thought of the Village. The interview questions are found in Appendix C.

For the most part, the competitors approached for interviews were quite willing to participate, and their responses were fairly candid. The following summarizes the findings from the interviews with Village competitors.

In comparison to other providers of intensive children's services and managed behavioral health services, the Village is characterized by the following **strengths**:

- ✔ Other providers do not appear to have a comparable continuum of care (except for managed behavioral health);

- ✔ The agency is moving forward with a strategic business approach, while other providers perceive the environment as noncompetitive;

- ✔ The agency's longevity has established a strong reputation in the local community;

- ✔ Quality staff work in the Village's programs;

- ✔ Diversity of staff is exemplified in bicultural and bilingual members; and

- ✔ Size of agency and diversity of programs.

In comparison to other providers of intensive children's services and managed behavioral health services, the Village displayed the following **weaknesses**:

- ✔ The Village is not well known among organizations located outside of Hartford—other providers do not recognize the Village as a competitor (especially in managed behavioral health).

- ✔ Some community-based agencies are beginning to diversify sources of revenue (e.g., fees, fundraising), a strategy the Village should consider. The Village's dependence on state funding and endowment places the agency at economic risk.

✔ The reliance on the state and the endowment as the major funding sources may limit the flexibility of the Village to rapidly respond to changes in the marketplace.

The consultant also conducted interviews with representatives from referring agencies and key funders. For the Village, this meant interviews with the local United Way and state child welfare department. While no gaps in services were identified, some of those interviewed mentioned the following areas as being underserved:

✔ Substance abuse services targeted to mothers and children (directly or indirectly involved);

✔ Parenting services (parenting education, parenting support and counseling, family communication);

✔ Afterschool programs for children (recreational, mental health);

✔ Transportation for afterschool services;

✔ Support and education on how to access the educational system; and

✔ Adoptive homes for children with special needs (physical, emotional, mental, sibling placements, children over age 8, minority children).

Agencies considered competitive to the Village were also identified during these interviews. The list was similar to the one drawn up earlier by the agency. It was encouraging to hear that the majority of those interviewed believe that, based on the scope and quality of services provided, the Village truly stands out from all other area providers. Both the staff and management of the Village are held in high regard. From their perspective, they identified the following Village **strengths**:

✔ The vision and leadership of Board and management (strength, innovation, openness);

✔ Creativity and willingness to work with families and other agencies to address a family's needs;

✔ Quality (skills, training, and commitment) of staff;

✔ Long-standing reputation and history of success/name recognition;

✔ Strength and quality of programs;

✔ Cultural competence of staff;

✔ Strong market presence/scope of services;

✔ Community-based services; and

✔ Flexibility and responsiveness to regional needs.

The following Village **weaknesses** were identified:

✔ Changes in the external environment, such as growth of managed care, may impact the future of the Village;

✔ "Size" of organization may inhibit sensitivity to client's needs (e.g., "needs to be more grassroots-oriented");

✔ Need "more efficient access" to specialized foster care; and

✔ Rate of pay for staff (too low—may encourage turnover).

Table 2 provides further detail on the Village's image from the perspective of the key funder and referring agency.

The competitive analysis concluded with the following recommendations for the future:

✔ The Village should continue its forward movement toward its visions,

✔ The Village should diversify its funding base,

✔ The Village should focus on improving its cost effectiveness,

Table 2. The Village for Families & Children Image Assessment

Characteristic	Average[*]	High[*]	Low[*]
Quality of programs and services	4.3	5	4
Innovation or "cutting edge" of programs	4.3	5	3
Quality of staff	4.4	5	4
Cultural diversity and sensitivity of staff	4.1	5	3
Strength of management	4.4	5	4
Strength of board leadership	4.4	5	4
Positive reputation in community	4.4	5	4
Cost effectiveness of services	3.8	5	3
Overall competitiveness	4.6	5	4

[*]On a scale of 1 to 5 (1=low; 5=high)

✔ The Village should continue with its efforts to design innovative programs,

✔ The Village should collaborate and coordinate with other agencies (especially in specialized foster care), and

✔ The Village should continue its open dialogue and communication with the key funders.

These broad recommendations were incorporated into the strategies developed as part of the business plan.

REFERENCES

Hinterhuber, H. H., & Popp, W. (1992, January/February). Are you a strategist or just a manager? *Harvard Business Review, 70*(1), 105-113.

Laufer, A. (1984). *Understanding your social service agency.* Newbury Park, CA: Sage.

Mockler, R. J. (1989). *Knowledge-based systems for strategic planning.* Englewood Cliffs, NJ: Prentice-Hall, Inc.

Moore, J. F. (1996*). The death of competition: Leadership and strategy in the age of business ecosystems.* New York: HarperCollins Publishers.

Oster, S. M. (1995). *Strategic management for nonprofit organizations: Theory and cases.* New York: Oxford University Press, Inc.

Pearce, J. A., & Robinson, R. B. (1994). *Strategic management: Formulation, implementation, and control* (5th ed.). Burr Ridge, IL: Irwin, Inc.

Weiner, M. (1982). *Human services management.* Homewood, IL: Dorsey Bess.

8 Allocating Discretionary Dollars

Many nonprofit organizations engage in fundraising activities to sustain or expand their efforts. In addition, some organizations also have endowment or trust funds they can draw from to support programs or other activities. If this pool of funds can be disbursed at the discretion of the organization, within predetermined parameters, then this is an effective tool for driving key strategies that otherwise are underfunded. As noted by David [1993], allocation of financial—as well as physical, human, and technological—resources is a key management activity that allows for strategy implementation.

Prior to the Village's strategic business planning, distribution of the agency's discretionary funds, primarily its endowment, was based in large part on historical patterns. For example, a service that received a particular amount of discretionary support continued to receive approximately the same level of funding the following year. The endowment was also used as a deficit funder. That is, a service that was unable to produce sufficient income to meet its projected expenses received supplemental support to close this gap.

As will be described in the next section, the Village took a more proactive stance on the use of its discretionary funds as part of its strategic business planning process. Rather than relying on history or deficit funding to guide how money was spent, the agency shifted to using endowment and charitable contributions as a first dollar investment in the agency's future. Thus, prior to developing department budgets, the agency's management determined the best strategic use of its discretionary funds. Management then based decisions on information and understanding of strategies, two factors that, when overlooked, frequently prevent effective resource allocation [Yavits & Newman 1982].

When this new methodology was first introduced, managers met it with both excitement and trepidation. The process about to be described, however, was endorsed by the agency's leadership team prior to implementation. Overall, managers and board members were pleased with the results.

The Village for Families & Children A sizable endowment is one of the Village's most valuable resources. Consequently, its distribution significantly impacts the direction of the agency. To best utilize this resource, it was decided that the Village's endowment distribution would meet the following goals:

✔ Create a means for applying endowment to a line of business, with appropriate leadership then determining the endowment for specific products;

✔ Provide the support needed to launch innovative new programs;

✔ Make available the investment capital needed to expand or enhance a promising service; and

✔ Apply endowment in a manner that does not return the Village to departmentalization and fragmentation.

The endowment allocation occurred in three steps, or levels:

✔ **Level 1:** percentage of endowment allocated to the four lines of business in investment capital, seed money, and value-added services;

✔ **Level 2:** percentage of endowment allocated to each of the lines of business; and

✔ **Level 3:** percentage of endowment allocated to the services within each line of business.

Endowment allocation decisions at Levels 1 and 2 were made by the Village's top management group, the CLT, using a voting process. Level 3 endowment allocation decisions were made by the Program Leadership Team members responsible for that line of business. The following sections describe each of these steps in detail. For demonstration purposes, the agency's line of business related to Intensive Children's Services (e.g., foster care, adoption, extended day treatment) is reported. Before reviewing the endowment allocation levels, some of the terms used are also defined.

One term used in the strategic business planning and endowment allocation process is **value-added service**. The value-added services consist of Research and Planning Services, the Grants Office, Training Services, and the agency's Library. These are called value-added services, because their purpose is to enhance quality or add value to the programs within the agency's four lines of business. Value-added services also promote the agency's ability to compete for funds and assure high-quality services. Each year a portion or percentage of the revenue available from the endowment is set aside to support research and training initiatives. Endowment allocated to this area is used to directly support the agency mission, strategic priorities, and strategic business plan.

The purpose of **investment capital** is to expand or enhance an existing service. Each year a portion or percentage of the revenue available from the endowment is set aside to support initiatives that are consistent with the strategic business plan of the Village. The initiatives funded may fall under the expense category of operating or capital, or both. Funds may be used to accelerate increases in market share through direct service products, mergers, or affiliations. To qualify for these funds, it must be demonstrated that the project will address an emerging market.

One example of such an initiative is to offer an existing service at a new site. Thus, not only are activities funded by investment capital consistent with the agency mission, vision, strategic priorities, operational strategies, and strategic business plan, they promote and position the Village.

From time to time the percentage guideline may be reconsidered, but unused dollars are not retained from one fiscal period to the next. Funds are awarded by the CLT. Operating awards are available for two years and capital awards for one year. Under limited circumstances, awards can be made prospectively. For example, money might be allocated for later use and linked to a merger or affiliation initiative. The funds are available to match other funds or to be the sole source of money to leverage position if there is assurance of other funds in the second year. The investment capital award is not intended to offset aggressive pursuit of outside funds. The Village President makes a full report to the Board of Directors on projects awarded funds and on their goal outcomes.

The purpose of **seed money** is for the development of new products. Each year a portion or percentage of the revenue from the endowment is set aside to support innovative new initiatives that are consistent with the agency mission, strategic priorities, operational strategies, and strategic business plan. One example of such an initiative is developing an intensive family preservation program.

Funds are awarded at any time during the fiscal period by the New Products Development Team for up to three years per project. The awards decrease to 66% of the original award in the second year and 33% of the original award in the third year. The funds are available to match other funds or to be the sole source of financing in order to leverage position, if there is assurance of other funds in the second and third year. From time to time, the percentage guidelines may be reconsidered. Unused project dollars are not retained from one fiscal period to the next. Note also that the seed money awards are not intended to offset aggressive pursuit of outside funds. The President makes a full report to the Board of Directors on projects awarded funds and on their goal outcomes.

It should be pointed out that these separate pools of money do not preclude the development of new products, or expansion or enhancement of existing products. These endeavors may also be financed by endowment earmarked for the line of business in the Level 2 endowment allocation.

To determine whether a request for seed money should be granted, guidelines for assessing proposed new products or services were developed. A New Product Development Team was formed to assess requests and report their findings to the CLT. The New Product Development Team Guidelines are presented at the end of this chapter on page 89.

LEVEL 1

Level 1 Endowment Allocation determines what percentage of endowment should be allocated to the four lines of business in total investment capital, seed money, and value-added services.

The percentage allocated to each of the four areas is determined by the CLT. Members individually vote by assigning a percentage to each of the four areas. The percentages must total to 100%. The arithmetic average percent assigned to each area is then computed. For example, the CLT recently agreed with the following Level 1 allocation:

	Endowmt + fundraising in FY96	Percent in FY96	Percent in FY97	Percent change from FY96	Endowmt + fundraising in FY97	$ Change from FY97
Lines of Business	$2,057,000	77.8%	76.75%	-1.1%	$2,126,743	$69,743
Investment Capital	$58,000	2.2%	3.08%	0.9%	$85,347	$27,347
Seed Money	0	0.0%	2.17%	2.2%	$60,131	$60,131
Value-Added Svcs	$529,000	20.0%	18.00%	-2.0%	$498,780	-$30,220
TOTAL	**$2,644,000**	**100%**	**100%**	--	**$2,771,000**	**$127,000**

LEVEL 2

Level 2 Endowment Allocation determines what percentage of the four lines of business in total is allocated to each line of business. For the Village, Level 2 allocation determined what percentage was allocated to Intensive Children's Services, Managed Behavioral Health

Services, Neighborhood and Family Strengthening Services, and Workplace Services.

Endowment allocation to the four lines was determined by a CLT voting process. Members assigned a percentage to each line of business using the following guidelines:

✔ In comparison to the previous fiscal year, the percentage of budgeted endowment could be raised or lowered by 5 percentage points (e.g., a 48% endowment allocation to the Intensive Children's Services in one fiscal year could be raised to a maximum of 53% or lowered to a minimum of 43% in the next fiscal year).

✔ The four percentages must total 100%.

✔ The voting occurred after CLT members had heard information on major trends, competitive analysis, internal assessment, and a presentation on a line's strategic options.

Ideally, there is consensus among CLT members on the final allocation recommendations. If consensus is not possible, then at least 10 out of the 12 CLT members need to be in support of the recommendations. The President and Executive Vice President then make the final recommendations to the Board of Directors in the annual budget approval meeting.

The Combined Leadership Team recently agreed with the following Level 2 Endowment Allocation results:

	Endowmt + fundraising in FY96	Percent in FY96	Percent in FY97	Percent change from FY96	Endowmt + fundraising in FY97	$ Change from FY97
Intensive Children's Svcs	$973,000	47.3%	49.65%	2.35%	$1,055,928	$82,928
Managed Behav. Health Svcs.	$848,000	41.23%	39.95%	-1.28%	$849,634	$1,634
Neighborhood & Family Svcs.	$196,000	9.53%	9.25%	-0.28%	$196,724	$724
Workplace Svcs.	$40,000	1.94%	1.15%	-0.79%	$24,458	-$15,542
TOTAL	**$2,057,000**	100%	100%	--	**$2,126,744**	**$69,744**

LEVEL 3

Level 3 Endowment Allocation determines how the endowment reserved for that particular line of business (from Level 2) will be used. Program Leadership Team members with responsibility for services within each line make this decision. The following is an example of recent voting results for Level 3 Endowment Allocation for the Intensive Children's Services line of business:

	Endowmt + fundraising in FY96	Percent in FY96	Percent in FY97	Percent change from FY96	Endowmt + fundraising in FY97	$ Change from FY97
Specialized Foster Care	$344,000	35.35%	45%	9.65%	$475,168	$131,168
Extended Day Treatment	$235,000	24.15%	34.5%	10.35%	$364,295	$129,295
STEP	0	0%	0%	0%	0	0
Intensive Family Preservation	$132,000	13.57%	0%	-13.57%	0	-$132,000
Adoption	$252,000	25.9%	20.5%	-5.4%	$216,465	-$35,535
Family Reunification	$10,000	1.03%	0%	-1.03%	0	-$10,000
TOTAL	$973,000	100%	100%	100%	$1,055,928	$82,928

By thoughtfully allocating an agency's discretionary funds at the beginning of the fiscal year, rather than as a deficit funder at the end of the year, the organization controls its destiny to the greatest extent possible.

GUIDELINES FOR NEW PRODUCT DEVELOPMENT

These guidelines are intended to ensure that new product development occurs in a fully integrated and coordinated fashion. Maximizing communication, interactive planning, and the development of fellowship is necessary to improve this process. These guidelines also bring a TQM approach to product development.

Listed below are the goals of new product development at the Village:

✔ Establish a balanced array of agency services along the continuum/systems of care (or lines of business).

✔ Decide who/which organizations it would be advantageous to collaborate with in order to
 - improve alignment with community-based services, and
 - improve alignment with financially viable services and expanding markets.

✔ Be responsive to our customers and consumers.

✔ Stay in business.

✔ Provide more efficient and effective prevention and intervention services.

Units of activity considered New Product Development include the following:

✔ Activities within an existing program that have never been offered before as a full program at the agency; and/or that have a specific budget and anticipated/actual funding source(s); including endowment, and with a specific staff allocation.

✔ Qualitative changes in activities that are so different as to result in a change in the service or program description/brochure, etc.

✔ Activities that have never been offered before at the agency; they may be a freestanding entity not part of any existing service or program currently at the agency.

Units of activity **not** considered New Product Development include the following:

✔ Quantitative change in activities—expanding the service to more clients without changing the targeted population.

✔ Minor qualitative change in activities that do not result in a change in the service or program description/brochure.

✔ A change/addition of a new funding source for activities that already exist at the agency.

Ideas for new products may be generated by one or more of the following constituents: leadership/management, staff, state child welfare agency, Board of Directors, clients, another organization that approaches the Village, affiliate organization, or community needs assessment/trends identification.

The New Product Development Team consists of the agency's Grants Officer and Senior Vice President of Research and Planning as standing committee members and two Program Leadership Team members and one Administrative Leadership Team member as rotating members. A line staff member with expertise in the proposed product area is on the team to review that particular product. The CLT annually appoints two Program Leadership Team members and one Administrative Leadership Team member to serve a six-month term on the New Product Development Team. Listed below are the responsibilities of the New Product Development Team:

✔ Receiving proposals for new product development needs and opportunities.

✔ Coordinating a feasibility study that includes
  - congruence with mission and strategic priorities;
  - fit with five operational strategies (see page 7);
  - community impact and contribution to future position;
  - relationship to gaps in continuum of care; and
  - internal impact of product on staff, budget, endowment, space, and liability.

✔ External impact of product on client needs and demand for service, funding opportunities, and income growth potential.

✔ Consultation with agency client advisory boards, appropriate Administrative Leadership Team members (e.g., Chief Financial Officer for budget implications, Senior Vice

President of Administrative Services for space implications, Vice President of Development and Communications for related fundraising), and relevant program staff.

✔ Producing a recommendation report for the Program Leadership Team, including the Grants Officer's view on funding opportunities.

✔ Advantages and disadvantages of doing, or not doing, the project.

✔ Team's recommendation to develop or not develop the product.

✔ Presenting a report to the Program Leadership Team.

The Product Champion(s) comes up with the idea for a new product. In this role, the Champion(s) will formally submit new product ideas to the New Product Development Team, be available to the team to answer questions, provide supporting information on an as-needed basis, and create enthusiasm and develop followers for the new product.

STEPS IN REVIEWING A NEW PRODUCT PROPOSAL

Step 1

The Product Champion (and planning group if already formed) will bring the product idea to the New Product Development Team. The information will be in the form of a feasibility checklist (see Table 3).

Step 2

The Village has a commitment to processing ideas for new products quickly and flexibly. The President, Executive Vice President, and any other interested CLT members will be invited to a meeting or consultation with the Champion/planning group and New Product Development Team. An overview of the proposed product will be given at the beginning of the meeting. If present, the President will

Table 3. Feasibility Study Checklist

Product Name: _____

Product Champion: _____

Is the proposed new product ...

Y N 1. congruent with our mission—to reverse the increase in violence and abuse affecting families in this generation?

Y N 2. congruent with our strategic priorities of substance abuse, violence, and child abuse and neglect?

Y N 3. a fit with our five operational strategies (be more responsive to our consumers, provide more community-based services, make every effort to empower agency clients and staff, encourage greater internal and external collaboration, provide holistic family services)?

Y N 4. an important contribution to future agency position and impact in the community?

Y N 5. helpful in filling gaps in our continuum of care/lines of business?

Y N 6. having a positive internal impact on staff?

Y N 7. having a positive internal impact on budget?

Y N 8. having a positive or neutral impact on endowment?

Y N 9. having a minimal impact on space?

Y N 10. having a minimal impact on liability?

Y N 11. having a minimal impact on the agency's management information system?

Y N 12. having a positive external impact on client needs and demand for service?

Y N 13. having a positive impact on the agency's market share within the relevant line of business?

Additional comments:

then offer his/her thoughts on how the proposed product fits with the global direction of the agency and raise any questions or concerns. The President may decide not to stay for the remainder of the meeting.

The meeting will take place in a timely fashion and the following factors will be explored in an oral feasibility study (minutes are taken to document the discussion):

- ✔ Congruence with mission and strategic priorities;
- ✔ Fit with five operational strategies;
- ✔ Community impact and contribution to future position;
- ✔ Relationship to gaps in continuum of care;
- ✔ Internal impact of product on staff, budget, endowment, space, liability, and management information system; and
- ✔ External impact of product on client needs and demand for service, funding opportunities, and income growth potential.

Step 3

A recommendation report is produced for the President and the Program Leadership Team. The report is based on the following information obtained primarily during the feasibility study:

- ✔ Input from consultation with agency:
  - Client advisory boards;
  - Appropriate Administrative Leadership Team members (e.g., Chief Financial Officer for budget implications);
  - Executive Vice President;
  - Senior Vice President of Administrative Services for space, liability, and management information system implications;
  - Vice President of Development and Communications for related fundraising; and

- Relevant program staff.

✔ Grants Officer's view on funding opportunities;

✔ Advantages and disadvantages of doing, or not doing, the project; and

✔ Team's recommendation to develop or not develop the product.

Step 4

The Program Leadership Team will be notified that a potential new product is ready for review. A meeting with the Program Leadership Team, Product Champion, and New Product Development Team will then be scheduled as soon as possible. If there is such a need, the report on the new product will be distributed and a meeting scheduled within 24 hours. The recommendation report is presented to the Program Leadership Team for review of recommendations of New Product Development Team and for reaching consensus or majority on a decision to proceed with the product. If the decision to proceed is not reached by a majority and the Product Champion disputes the decision with a compelling argument, then the product design may be revised and reviewed again by the Program Leadership Team.

Step 5

The Executive Vice President's signature indicates Program Leadership Team consensus/approval to develop the product.

Step 6

The President then does a final review and sign-off. The President also determines what possible action is required of the Board of Directors. Informational reports are provided to the appropriate board committees and task forces. If the go-ahead is given, then Step 7 occurs (however, due to time constraints, preliminary work may commence prior to the formal approval).

Step 7

A subgroup of the New Product Development Team forms to work on actual development of the product. This subgroup is responsible for the following:

- ✔ A plan is devised for the new product development,

- ✔ The Champion acts as the liaison between this subgroup and the Program Leadership Team to report progress on development of the product,

- ✔ The new product is launched/plan is implemented, and

- ✔ The Champion provides progress updates to the Program Leadership Team.

The New Product is then monitored, with evaluation reports being provided periodically to the Program Leadership Team. The New Product Development Team reviews the product with the Champion after a mutually agreed-upon time has passed. A recommendation is then made to continue, revise, or discontinue the new product. This recommendation is shared with the Program Leadership Team. This review continues until the effort is no longer considered a new product.

REFERENCES

David, F. R. (1993). *Strategic management* (4th ed.). New York: Macmillan Publishing Company.

Yavits, B., & Newman, W. (1982). *Strategy in action: The execution, politics, and payoff of business planning.* New York: The Free Press.

9 Developing and Implementing Strategies

The culmination of all this careful planning is the selection and implementation of strategies that will promote and strengthen the organization. Bryson [1995] defines a strategy as "a pattern of purposes, policies, programs, actions, decisions, or resource allocations that define what an organization is, what it does, and why it does it" (p. 32).

Strategy selection is influenced by the opportunities available at the time of decision making. Referred to as strategic windows, there are limited time periods when an organization can use its current competencies to optimally take advantage of an opportunity, or open windows [Abell 1978].

Strategies are developed at several different levels:

✔ For the organization overall,

✔ For the line of business, and

✔ For the program or service.

The process for selecting strategies is essentially the same at each of the three levels but may vary, however, in the personnel involved in strategy selection. Managers, representative staff members, community leaders, partners, and clients, for example, may play a role in determining the overall strategies, while a mix of leaders and staff within a particular line of business may participate in the line of business strategy selection. Similarly, program staff and leaders will most likely select the strategies for their service or program.

STEPS FOR SELECTING STRATEGIES

The steps taken to select strategies at any of the three levels are quite similar. Following is an outline of the steps that may be used to select strategies for a line of business.

Step 1

Have the line of business leader or coordinator convene the work group, including line staff and management. Two half-day sessions will most likely be needed to work through the process. Any preparation done in advance of the meeting—particularly with regard to Step 2—will be beneficial to completing the work in a timely way.

Step 2

As preparation, read over the line of business vision. Then brainstorm possible strategic options by using the following six questions to generate ideas:

1. What new strategies could be employed to further the line of business vision?

2. Consider advantages over the competition and where competitors are weak. Then answer the question, "What new things can the line do to capitalize on our advantages over the competition and areas where our competitors are weak?"

3. Consider the line of business strengths as perceived by clients and consumers, program staff, and funders and customers. Then answer the question, "What strategies could be employed to capitalize on these strengths?"

4. Consider the line of business weaknesses as perceived by clients and consumers, program staff, and funders and customers. Then answer the question, "What strategies could be employed to lessen or address these weaknesses or liabilities?"

5. Consider what additional funding sources might be available. Then answer the question, "Is there anything about these additional funding sources that suggests strategies to further the line?"

6. What other strategies have not yet been mentioned?

These six questions may be answered using the following structure:

✔ Take each question separately,

✔ Have each person individually write down her/his thoughts to the question,

✔ Use a round-robin format to get all unique ideas on flipchart,

✔ Have some discussion to clarify what is meant rather than to debate an idea's merit,

✔ Proceed to the next question, and

✔ Repeat the procedure.

Step 3

Select strategic options for the next six to 12 months. Because it is not possible to adopt all the ideas, the work team will need to select the strategies they believe are *key* to achieving the line of business vision.

It is up to the work group to determine how they wish to narrow the list of options. One way to get a quick sense of where the group is, is to have participants individually write their top ideas on paper. The voting results can then be listed on a flipchart and debated by the group. During the debate, the following questions might be considered:

✔ Does the strategy further the agency mission?

✔ Does the strategy fit with the line of business vision?

✔ How does this strategy impact the line of business? Other lines of business?

✔ What sort of contribution would this strategy make to future positioning of the organization?

✔ What positive impact would this strategy have on the community?

✔ What negative impact would this strategy have on the community?

✔ Is the strategy a major initiative or a more modest action?

✔ Is the list balanced, or are there too many major initiatives?

To further test the feasibility of the strategies and reduce them to a manageable number, consider the following:

✔ What resources would the strategy require?
- Staff
- Space
- Support services
- Technology
- Capital resources
- Marketing needs

✔ Would the strategy involve a major staffing change?

✔ Would the strategy involve staff reassignment?

✔ If more staff are required, could they come from another line of business?

✔ How would the strategy be funded?

✔ Who would the collaborators be—both internal and external—on this strategy?

Step 4

Identify the lead person and others who will work on each strategy. One individual should be responsible for making sure that a GANTT chart is completed as implementation of the strategy progresses. The lead person will convene meetings and periodically report progress to the leadership team.

Step 5

Develop a GANTT Chart for each strategy, detailing the key activities and associated timeframes. An example of a GANTT Chart is provided on page 103.

The Village for Families & Children | The Village went through a process similar to the one just described. Line of business work groups convened meetings to select strategies to implement in the upcoming fiscal year. The groups each began with a review of the line of business vision and aspects of the situational assessment and competitive analysis relevant to the strategy selection. For example, one of the six strategy stimulation questions reviewed earlier suggested that the line of business strengths be considered from the perspective of clients and consumers, program staff, and funders and customers. There were several questions on the staff self-assessment survey that spoke to these considerations. Similarly, another one of the six questions related to the competitive analysis and what new things the line could do to capitalize on the organization's advantages over the competition and areas where competitors are weak.

Using a flipchart, the groups brainstormed a list of possible strategies. After much discussion, the list was narrowed through a voting process. The remaining strategies were then subjected to a feasibility study, assessing such factors as contribution to future positioning of the Village, strategy funding, and impact on the community and line of business. For example, an idea might have been eliminated if, after much discussion, the work group felt that implementing the strategy would have a negative impact on the community.

Approximately four to six strategies were selected for each line of business. Lead persons, often participants from the work group, were identified for each strategy. Line staff also participated in the strategy development and implementation, forming a small team or committee. Line staff were recruited during strategic business plan presentations where results were shared, or were approached by the strategy's lead person.

A GANTT chart was then produced, usually by the lead person, in consultation with the other members working on the strategy. An example of a GANTT chart for a strategy from the Intensive Children's Services line of business is given in Figure 2.

A similar process was followed to establish agencywide objectives. The Village's management team selected six agencywide objectives for implementation during a recent fiscal year. The agencywide business strategies are quite broad, pertaining to the entire organization. Some of the agencywide objectives selected had been identified as priorities by the management team before the strategic business planning process. Folding those strategies into the current effort assured that they would not be lost during this new round of planning.

Implementation plans for each of these strategies were developed by the manager responsible for the effort. The strategies were monitored during the 12-month period immediately following approval of the strategic business plan. Listed below are the agencywide strategies:

- ✔ Develop and implement a comprehensive marketing plan to effectively market agency services (including managed care and identifying outcomes that are managed care friendly);

- ✔ Attain uniformity in agency record keeping (including integration in automation efforts);

- ✔ Establish an Agencywide Group Program;

- ✔ Develop and implement strategies to enhance and maintain cultural competency (including exploration of use of the CWLA cultural competency instrument);

Figure 2. Strategic Business Plan GANTT Chart for Line of Business

Activity	Q4 (FY 96)			Q1 (FY 97)			Q2 (FY 97)			Q3 (FY 97)			Q4 (FY 97)		
	Apr	May	June	Jul	Aug	Sept	Oct	Nov	Dec	Jan	Feb	Mar	Apr	May	June
A. Revise budget	■														
B. Negotiate new timetable for program operations	■														
C. Begin renovations to "STEP" Building		■		■											
D. Hire and train program staff		■													
1. Designate one Specialized Foster Care staff member to be a liaison to the STEP program.															
2. Designate two Specialized Foster Care staff as caseworkers															
3. Provide STEP orientation for all three Specialized Foster Care staff and identify and clarify roles and responsibilities					■	■									
E. Have managed care VP begin marketing program to managed care companies				■	■	■									
F. Begin operation of program					■										
G. Hold six-month review of STEP Team functioning											■				
H. Hold annual review of program, including collaboration efforts.														■	

✔ Strengthen advocacy efforts of the agency (including linkage/coordination with the Board Public Issues Committee); and

✔ Expand the Village's client-driven/responsive efforts (including feasibility of establishing an agencywide Client Advisory Board).

STRATEGY IMPLEMENTATION

Although the strategic business planning process strives to account for as many opportunities and possibilities as is imaginable, it is still difficult to anticipate the future. Thus, the actual implementation will be a blend of planned strategies, as well as actions that take advantage of unplanned opportunities [Mintzberg 1994].

It is not atypical for aspects of implementation to begin prior to completion of the plan [Bryson 1995]. The GANTT chart provided on page 103 has activities that began prior to the start of the fiscal year. A weakness that is particularly damaging to the organization can, and should, be remedied quickly. However, if the planning process becomes derailed as information is unearthed or highlighted at each step in the planning, then a full understanding of the composite organization cannot be appreciated and utilized for comprehensive strategy development.

The implementation plans associated with each strategic objective were captured in the GANTT charts. The GANTT charts provided direction and were an aid for each leader's individual planning. They were not considered to be cast in stone and were modified as new information became available and experiences and events occurred.

REFERENCES

Abell, D. F. (1978, Fall). Strategic windows. *Journal of Marketing*, 21-26.

Bryson, J. M. (1995). *Strategic planning for public and nonprofit organizations: A guide to strengthening and sustaining organizational achievement.* San Francisco: Jossey-Bass Publishers.

Mintzberg, H. (1994). *The rise and fall of strategic planning.* New York: Free Press.

10 Monitoring the Implementation Plan

Monitoring is essential to gain a clear picture of the progress that is made in implementing these carefully crafted strategies. The authors have found that the very act of monitoring also influences the rate of progress to a certain extent, motivating those responsible for implementation to make progress so that they may recount it in the upcoming monitoring report. Scheduled updates remind leaders of commitments made earlier to advance a particular strategy.

When considering monitoring, there are two questions that need to be answered: How will the monitoring be done? and How often will the monitoring occur? With regard to how the monitoring will be done, there are several pieces of information that should be collected:

✔ Who is involved in implementing the strategy?

✔ Has the personnel or leadership changed since the last reported update?

✔ Should additional staff be added to the effort at this point in implementing the strategy?

For example, if the strategy to be implemented relates to adding a short-term emergency placement program, then intake workers might be involved in developing the admission protocol, and specialized foster care staff might be involved in developing the process and criteria for referring children into the short-term emergency placement program, as well as for exiting the program and entering a foster home placement.

It is important to view the monitoring of the strategic business plan in a positive light. Rather than considering it a burden or a time when lack of progress is exposed, Brady [1984] suggests that participants understand that slower-than-anticipated progress is not necessarily due to their performance. Barriers, or factors beyond the individuals' control, are another piece of information that should be collected during the strategic business plan monitoring. While it is easy for those implementing the plan to feel defensive or disappointed about slower-than-expected progress, it is also realistic to expect barriers outside of their control to impede progress. Following are some examples of barriers to strategy implementation:

- ✔ Delays in areas of implementation that are the responsibility of collaborating partners;

- ✔ Changes that occur with collaborating organizations, which result in changes to original agreements or commitments made to the agency;

- ✔ Changes in the population from which clients would be expected to come;

- ✔ Lack of time to devote to strategy implementation, due to unexpected pressing issues; and

- ✔ Need to clarify roles and responsibilities in new relationships among two or more agency programs.

Overall, when considering how the monitoring will be done, the "keep it simple" rule should be enforced. As David [1993] notes, the test of an effective monitoring system is not its complexity, but rather, its usefulness. A general understanding of progress made since the last monitoring update could be as simple as assigning a progress rating to the strategy. For example, the following rating system might be adopted:

Rating   Phase/Status

1   Have not yet started to address this strategic objective.

2   Are in the early planning/development stage.

3   Would say we are in an advanced stage of development and pos-
sibly early implementation.

4   Have implemented/accomplished/completed the strategic objective.

5   Chose to abandon the strategic objective.

In addition to the progress rating, a review of the GANTT chart is also useful in showing where and when slippage has occurred and how modifications will affect the remainder of the strategy implementation activities. If the changes are great, then a revised GANTT chart would be called for. As noted in Chapter 9, the GANTT charts are not cast in stone, and modifications are quite permissible.

There are two schools of thought with regard to how frequently the monitoring should occur. Lindsay and Rue [1980] initially proposed that strategy evaluation occur less frequently for stable organizations and more frequently for organizations experiencing greater environmental changes and instability. Their research findings found just the opposite to occur, however, and they concluded that there is less need for frequent monitoring in unstable situations, because forecasting is more difficult and the strategies quickly become obsolete. Although forecasting may be difficult during turbulent times, an argument might be made for more frequent progress reports to remain current and informed of the changes and divergence from the initial strategy. The reports also serve as a record, and perhaps as educational tools, for future strategy implementation planning.

The Village for Families & Children Monitoring of the strategic business plan was initiated several months after the start of plan implementation. Monitoring occurred at several levels, corresponding to the three strategy levels. Thus, the agencywide strategies for the organization overall were monitored by the Combined Leadership Team; the line of business strategies were monitored by the Program Leadership Team; and the smaller, program, or service strategies were monitored by the key program leaders and staff in that particular area.

The Program Leadership Team reviewed the strategies for the four lines of business, as well as the value-added services, on a quarterly basis. During the reviews, the program leaders with responsibility for that particular strategy were asked to report on progress since the last quarterly update. The leader responsible was first asked to clarify any changes in the personnel working on implementation. As it was a goal of the strategic business planning to include line staff in the implementation phase, leaders were expected to identify program staff who were working on the strategy, in addition to themselves.

Next, the program leader responsible was asked to describe activities that had occurred since the last update. These activities had, for the most part, been outlined in the GANTT chart developed for the strategy. Variances were explained as well as slippages in the schedule of planned activities. An overall rating was given to progress on implementing the strategy. Using the five-point rating scale described on page 109, the program leader rated progress from 1, meaning he/she had not yet started to address the strategic objective, to 4, meaning the strategy had been fully implemented or achieved. A rating of 5 was only given one time, for a strategy that had been abandoned.

The program leader responsible for the strategy also identified barriers, if any. The barriers that impeded progress ranged from changes in the population from which clients would be expected to come to a lack of time to work on strategy implementation.

To summarize progress in one of the quarters, 30 strategies were identified within the four lines of business and value-added services. At the time of the review, only one strategy had been abandoned and progress had been made on all but one of the remaining 29 strategies. A total of seven, or 23%, of the strategies had been accomplished, and another 12, or 40%, were in an advanced stage of development or early implementation. Barriers were identified for less than half the strategies. Barriers included a lack of time to work on implementation and delays in areas of implementation that were the responsibility of collaborating partners.

REFERENCES

Brady, T. (1984). Six step method to long range planning for nonprofit organizations. *Managerial Planning, 32* (4), 49.

David, F. R. (1993). *Strategic management* (4th ed.). New York: Macmillan Publishing Company.

Lindsay, W., & Rue, L. (1980). Impact of the organization environment on the long-range planning process: A contingency view. *Academy of Management Journal. 23* (3), 402.

11 Refreshing the Strategic Business Plan

The organization must reexamine its plan on a periodic basis. Does it still make sense? Are these still the right strategies? Have changes occurred in the organization's external environment or in funder policies? Have there been unanticipated events or opportunities that should influence the course of the agency? The organization's planning team should sit down and review the strategic business plan annually, or more frequently, depending upon the need.

As noted by David [1993], every organization should take care not to become a prisoner of its own strategies, as all strategies eventually become obsolete. Hamermesh [1986] further points out that strategies are constantly being changed and revised as new threats and opportunities arise, and strategy development and implementation should be viewed as continuous and symbiotic.

In examining the Mission, ask these questions: Is this the right mission for the organization? Has there been difficulty tying actions to this mission?

In examining the Vision, ask these questions: What steps have been made to realize the organization's vision? The line of business visions? Is the agency any closer to the vision than when it was first developed?

In examining the Situational Assessment, ask these questions: Have there been significant internal changes in the organization? Have new strengths arisen that can become core competencies, to be drawn upon again and again? Have weaknesses come to light since the planning process, and if so, what corrections can be made to bolster those weaknesses?

In examining the External Assessment, keep in mind that the world surrounding the agency is changing. This is probably the area where the organization has the least amount of control. A funder may make a major, unanticipated change that heavily impacts key funding streams for the organization. The agency has to respond and ask these questions: Was there any way these events could have been anticipated? What strategy or process can be put in place to further monitor future "unanticipated actions" by the external environment, so that they can become more anticipated, or fewer in number?

In examining the Competitive Analysis, ask these questions: Have dominant competitors emerged that threaten the health of the organization? Have new agencies started competing for the same small pot of money? Are existing competitors expanding at an alarming rate?

In examining the Strategies, ask these questions: Are these still the right strategies? Has the agency strayed from the original intent due to unforeseen circumstances? Are these still the right strategies for the organization and the current world around it?

In examining the Financial Pro Formas, remember the financial projections and estimates that were made. Ask these questions: Has the agency been able to stick pretty close to these estimates, or have there been wide variances? Are there lines of business that are struggling financially? Does the agency need to make changes for the health of the organization as a whole?

The questions in each of these areas should be addressed during a group discussion among agency leaders. Answering these questions will help to structure the discussion and make the meeting time as productive and thorough as possible.

Leaders with responsibility for the services within the line of business should also convene meetings to refresh the strategies. If available, line staff from the original work group should also participate in these meetings. Similar to the original selection and development of the line of business strategies, the following steps may be used to structure the group's discussion during the refreshing of the line of business strategies. (The organization's leadership should follow similar steps to refresh and update the agencywide strategies.)

STEP 1

Convene the line of business work group, including line staff and leadership members. A full morning or afternoon will most likely be needed to refresh the line of business aspects of the strategic plan. As was the case for the initial set of such meetings to establish the strategies, any preparation done in advance of the meeting—particularly with regard to Step 2—will be especially important to completing the work in a timely way.

STEP 2

Brainstorm new strategic options. Read over the line of business vision and then answer the following six questions:

1. What new strategies could be employed to further the line of business vision?

2. Consider advantages over the competition and where competitors are weak. Then answer the question, "What new things can the line do to capitalize on our advantages over the competition and areas where our competitors are weak?"

3. Consider the line of business strengths as perceived by clients and consumers, program staff, and funders and customers. Then answer the question, "What strategies could be employed to capitalize on these strengths?"

4. Consider the line of business weaknesses as perceived by clients and consumers, program staff, and funders and customers. Then answer the question, "What strategies

could be employed to lessen or address these weaknesses or liabilities?"

5. Consider what additional funding sources might be available. Then answer the question, "Is there anything about these additional funding sources that suggests strategies to further the line?"

6. What other strategies have not yet been mentioned?

As was done in the initial brainstorming of strategies, the suggested format is to:

✔ take each question separately,

✔ have each person individually write down his or her thoughts to the question,

✔ use a round-robin format to get all unique ideas on flipchart,

✔ have some discussion to clarify what is meant rather than to debate an idea's merit,

✔ proceed to the next question, and

✔ repeat the procedure.

STEP 3

Select new strategic options for the upcoming fiscal year. Because it is not possible to adopt all the ideas, the work team will need to select the strategies they believe are *key* to achieving the line of business vision.

As was the case in the original strategy selection, it is up to the work group to determine how they wish to narrow the list of options. Through a voting process, individuals may select the ideas they like best.

Feasibility of potential strategies may be further tested by considering the resources the strategy would require, its possible contribution to agency positioning, impact on the community, etc.

STEP 4

Select current strategies that will be continued into the upcoming fiscal year. Review the line of business strategies as outlined in the current strategic business plan. Discuss the strategies that have not yet been fully implemented and make a determination as to whether they should be continued into the upcoming fiscal year.

STEP 5

Identify the lead person and others who will work on each strategy.

STEP 6

Complete a GANTT chart for each strategy, detailing the key activities and associated timeframes.

In summary, the time given to careful planning will provide a return to the organization that is well worth the investment. Strategic business planning is an effective way to secure the future of the nonprofit organization. There is no better time than now to begin this important endeavor.

REFERENCES

David, F. R. (1993). *Strategic management* (4th ed.). New York: Macmillan Publishing Company.
Hamermesh, R. G. (1986). *Making strategy work: How senior managers produce results.* New York: John Wiley & Sons, Inc.

A Internal Service Assessment Instrument

SERVICE DESCRIPTION

1. What is your service's mission or goal(s)?

2. What types of services and treatment modalities are offered?

3. Location of service distribution (sites)?

4. How has your service changed over the past five years and what caused these changes (e.g., changes in the target population)?

5. How do you measure the success or quality of your service and how successful is your service (e.g., use of client satisfaction measures)?

Description of Organization and Staff

6. How many staff does your service have, and what are their roles?

7. How diverse are staff (e.g., culturally, sex, bilingual, etc.)?

8. Does staff race/ethnicity affect your service's ability to attract and retain clients?

9. What is the staff organizational structure? How are staff supervised (by whom, how often)?

10. How are cases and duties assigned to staff?

11. What training is available to staff?

Service Funding and Cost

12. How are fees for clients determined and communicated?

13. What problems exist regarding fee collection?

14. How does funding affect the service's (and agency's) mission?

15. What additional funding sources might be available?

16. What changes have there been in the past three to five years in the way your service is funded?

17. How are service costs determined?

18. How cost effective is your service?

CLIENTS OR CONSUMERS

1. Who are the people who are buying from you? *(This information was provided by the automated management information system.)*
   - gender
   - age
   - income
   - marital status
   - education
   - family size

2. How can we find more people like these?

3. How would you characterize your markets?

4. What barriers prevent potential customers from receiving your service? How could you make it easier for customers to buy from you?

PRODUCT BENEFITS/SHORTFALLS

1. Why do our clients come to us for service?

2. Why do they come to us and not to the competition?

3. What are your service's strengths as perceived by clients/consumers?

4. What are your service's weaknesses (criticisms) as perceived by clients/consumers?

5. What are your service's strengths as perceived by program staff?

6. What are your service's weaknesses as perceived by program staff?

7. What are your service's strengths as perceived by funders/customers?

8. What are your service's weaknesses as perceived by funders/customers?

9. What internal and external constraints do service staff face in providing services (i.e., job stress factors, equipment needs, etc.)?

COMPETITION

1. Who are your primary current competitors and why?

2. What do your competitors do better than you (their strengths)?

3. What do your competitors do less well than you (their weaknesses)?

4. How do they please their customers?

5. What is their pricing policy?

6. Where and how do they advertise—and does it work?

7. Who are your emerging competitors?

8. Who are your potential competitors?

9. Who were your previous competitors, and why are they no longer competitors?

B Excerpts from the Internal Assessment Summary for Intensive Children's Services

Question	Extended Day Treatment	Specialized Foster Care	Intensive Family Preservation	Adoption
1. Service mission/goal	To provide comprehensive, intensive, clinical treatment services to children who exhibit emotional and behavioral problems in order to stabilize and improve their adaptive functioning, thereby decreasing the risk of out-of-home or community placement.	To provide healing family life for abused children threatened by placement in institutional care.	Intensive time-limited, home-based program that provides support and therapeutic services to Hartford families with at least one child at imminent risk of placement in foster, group, or institutional care. Currently, the program is piloting and evaluating two models of intensive family preservation services that vary from 12 to 26 weeks. The goals of the Intensive Family Preservation Program are to avert the threatened placement by reducing the risk of further harm to children and improving family functioning.	Permanently place special needs children in adoptive homes to interrupt cycle of abuse, violence, and neglect. **Note:** Special needs may be older children; drug and alcohol affected; physically, sexually, and emotionally abused; physically challenged; and/or learning disabled.
2. Types of services and treatment modalities offered	The following service and treatment modalities for children, ages 5 through 12, and their families: • Individual and group therapy • Parent and family therapy • Psychological testing and evaluation	• Specialized foster care, therapy, case management • In-home child behavioral therapy • Initial and ongoing training to foster families • 24-hour emergency and crisis support to foster families	• 5-20 hours per week of supportive home-based counseling and the provision of hard goods such as food, clothing, furniture, etc. • Crisis intervention, behavioral modification, and structural family therapy	• Recruit, study, and license adoptive families • Provide preplacement, placement, and postplacement and finalization services for children and families • Full range of search services for Adoption Triad

Question	Extended Day Treatment	Specialized Foster Care	Intensive Family Preservation	Adoption
2. Types of services and treatment modalities offered (continued)	• Behavioral motivational system • Psychiatric evaluation and consultation • Pediatric nurse consultation • Home-based parent advocate service • Case management involving such activities as school consultation, aftercare planning, and permanency planning • Bilingual (English and Spanish) services • Multicultural staff • Year-round programming and services, including a summer enrichment program • Transportation for children and parents • Structured afternoon and evening activities involving arts, recreation, tutoring, and cultural activities. • Children's computer lab	• Financial per diem to cover child expenses • Reimbursement for foster family mileage, baby-sitting during training, and a few specific additional items • Respite resources to foster family • Family therapy and reunification work when indicated • Permanency planning • Coordination with DCF and outside systems • Licensing and relicensing of families • Child treatment groups • Monthly foster parents support group • Recruitment, screening, and initial assessment of prospective families • Highly adaptive, creative, individualized treatment services to meet specific child and family needs (i.e., wraparound)	• Transportation • Household management • Child care skills • Educational information vis à vis eviction, housing problems, and relocation services • Discharge planning and referrals to support groups and/or other programs prior to termination	• Nonidentifying medical, reunion registry, and search • Unplanned pregnancy services • Counseling, placement services, postplacement, temporary foster care

Question	Extended Day Treatment	Specialized Foster Care	Intensive Family Preservation	Adoption
13. Why clients come to VFC	• DCF prefers to refer clients to us because we have the largest program in this region, and we offer a comprehensive, culturally diverse and clinically sound program • Continuum of care at the agency with such programs as Specialized Foster Care, Outpatient, Wraparound, and Family Reunification offers a comprehensive array of services that support treatment for entire family who are under protective services	• Our service provides good homes for difficult children (stable placements) • Therapy services for children • Family services for biological families of children • Sometimes our ability to match in certain location (worker requests home in or out of specific community) • Sometimes our ability to coordinate service, such as Extended Day Treatment and SFC	• Client families referred by DCF, however, are only provided after clients' families agree to accept recommended services	• High-quality, experienced staff • Cultural diversity • Commitment, flexibility, advocacy, family empowerment, collateral and collaborative initiatives • One worker from beginning to end of process • Collaboration with border states, excellent teamwork
14. Advantage over competition	• Have the largest program in this region • Offer a comprehensive, culturally diverse, and clinically sound program • Continuum of care at the agency	• Because we offer therapy services as part of the package • Because of the reputation of our homes • We give a quick response and often have the ability to begin service before others • Because we have more Hispanic homes, can make cultural/ethnic and other matches	• DCF referrals are based on availability of IFP therapists	• The most comprehensive services pre-, post-, and legalization • Adoption fees are highly competitive • Staff is sensitive and treat clients with dignity and respect

Question	Extended Day Treatment	Specialized Foster Care	Intensive Family Preservation	Adoption
19. Service weaknesses — per staff	• Child-to-staff ratio too high • Lack of clinical sophistication by Child Development Staff • Overuse of time-outs and not enough individual motivators by Child Development Specialist • Not enough psychiatric consultation time • Parent advocates need more training and supervision • Not enough bilingual staff • Foster parents cannot be forced to attend therapy/participate adequately in child's treatment	• Not enough team time • Space problems • Need for more cars and transportation resources • Not enough money for salaries when compared to DCF workers • Slow agency orientation from time of joining program makes it difficult to understand larger agency • Insufficient training for new staff, given the complexity of service demands Problems as perceived by foster parents who are not staff, but part of the service providers: • Not enough money • Not enough child care supports, especially to handle emergencies such as when a child is expelled from school	• Number of IFP therapists is viewed by staff as a weakness	• Lack of upward mobility • Lack of financial reward based on complexity and demands of service • Lack of vehicles • Lack of supportive services

C Interview Questions for the Competitive Analysis

1. Are you affiliated/do you collaborate with another organization?
2. Do you have any other locations? If yes, address:
3. What is your target client population?
4. What types of services do you offer?
5. How many clients do you see per week/month?
6. Has your volume increased or decreased over the last three years?
7. On average, how many visits per client do you normally provide/require?
8. Do you have a waiting list for services? How long?
9. What geographic area do you generally draw your cases from? What percentage of your total clients do you get from this area?
10. Do you anticipate expanding your geographic coverage? What will guide your decision?
11. Please describe your staffing by full- and part-time and profession.
12. Who are other providers of similar services in your area?
13. Who do you consider your chief competitors?
14. If the Village is one of your competitors, what do you think are its strengths? Its weaknesses?
15. As you look to the future, what are the three major concerns or critical issues affecting your organization?
16. What services/products do you have that you will eliminate, downsize, or anticipate difficulties in sustaining?
17. From your view, what are key services/products your organization should be involved in now?
18. What new services are you thinking of offering?

19. What do you consider to be your strengths?
20. Based on current trends and anticipated future needs of your clients, do you anticipate affiliating/collaborating with other providers? If yes, which organizations would you consider?
21. What is the cost for services?
22. What is your fee structure?
23. In response to managed care penetration of the market, have you contracted with any managed care companies? If yes, which companies?

About the Authors

Miriam P. Kluger, who holds a Ph.D. in applied psychological research and evaluation from Hofstra University, Hempstead, NY, is Senior Vice President for Research and Planning at the Village for Families and Children, Inc., Hartford, CT. Before joining the Village staff she was a health care analyst at Queens Hospital Community Mental Health Center in Jamaica, NY, and held management positions in project management training and public relations research at AT&T Communications, NJ. She is a member of the National Council on Research in Child Welfare and is the co-author of *Innovative Leadership in the Nonprofit Organization: Strategies for Change.*

William A. Baker is President of the Village for Families and Children, Inc., Hartford, CT, and former executive director of the Family and Children's Service Society of Summit County, Akron, OH. He earned his M.S.W. at the University of Michigan, Ann Arbor, MI. A member of the CWLA National Advisory Council and the steering committee for the CWLA North Atlantic Region, he also sits on the board of Family Service America, chairs the United Way Executive's Forum, and serves on the Connecticut Governor's Task Force on Adoption. He is also the co-author of *Innovative Leadership in the Nonprofit Organization: Strategies for Change.*

Howard S. Garval is Executive Vice President of the Village for Families and Children, Inc., Hartford, CT, and former district director, Group Treatment Coordinator and Clinical Social Worker at Family Service of Greater Boston. He earned his M.S.W. from the University of Michigan. He chaired the Managed Care Task Force for the CT Council of Family Service Agencies and has served as cochair of the Education and Legislative Action Network for NASW-CT, in addition to serving on the board, on the personnel committee, and on the strategic planning committee of that organization.

Innovative Leadership in the Nonprofit Organization: Strategies for Change

Miriam P. Kluger
William A. Baker

The nonprofits that will survive into the 21st century are those that can predict community needs and priorities and respond with the right services at the right price. This book outlines strategies for managing change in nonprofit organizations drawn from the authors' experiences in a large New England community agency serving children and families. These are strategies for change necessitated by shifting social, economic, political, and technological forces influencing the mission, direction, and financial viability of community services organizations.

To Order: 1994/0-87868-567-7   Stock #5677 $22.95

Write: CWLA c/o PMDS   Call: 800/407-6273
        P.O. Box 2019   301/617-7825
        Annapolis Junction, MD 20701
e-mail: cwla@pmds.com   Fax: 301/206-9789

Please specify stock #5677. Bulk discount policy (not for resale): 10-49 copies 10%, 50-99 copies 20%, 100 or more copies 40%. Canadian and foreign orders must be prepaid in U.S. funds. MasterCard/Visa accepted.

Quality-Centered/ Team-Focused Management

John Hodge-Williams
Joy F. Spratley Wynn
Cheryl Mason Godsey

With the nationwide implementation of managed care and the eroding financial base for children's services, agencies need new organizational systems to survive. This handbook provides an overview of one new system, Total Quality Management (TQM), as it relates to the child welfare field. The chapters cover such topics as customer service, leadership, teamwork, and quality improvement. In the last chapters of this useful guide, the authors present a TQM work process analysis, discuss how TQM is accomplished within an agency, and describe the specific steps in the TQM process.

To Order: 1998/0-87868-636-3 — Stock #6363 $18.95

Write: CWLA c/o PMDS
P.O. Box 2019
Annapolis Junction, MD 20701
e-mail: cwla@pmds.com

Call: 800/407-6273
301/617-7825

Fax: 301/206-9789

Please specify stock #6363. Bulk discount policy (not for resale): 10-49 copies 10%, 50-99 copies 20%, 100 or more copies 40%. Canadian and foreign orders must be prepaid in U.S. funds. MasterCard/Visa accepted.